The Many Flavors of Panna Cotta

Vanilla Bean Panna Cotta with Balsamic
Strawberries · page 21 ·

Toasted Coconut Panna Cotta
· page 26 ·

PB & J Panna Cotta
· page 23 ·

Coffee Toffee Panna Cotta
· page 27 ·

Lemon-Buttermilk Panna Cotta with
Crushed Raspberry Sauce · page 24 ·

Lavender Panna Cotta
with Blueberry Coulis · page 28 ·

Cappuccino
Layered
Panna Cotta
· page 30 ·

Chestnut Caramel Panna Cotta
· page 48·

Rocky Road Panna Cotta
· page 34 ·

Persian-Spiced Panna Cotta
with Candied Rose Petals · page 51 ·

Neapolitan
Panna Cotta
· page 41 ·

Five-Spice & Honey Panna Cotta
· page 52 ·

Cannoli Panna Cotta
· page 44 ·

Yogurt Panna Cotta
with Poached Apricots · page 64 ·

Maple Panna Cotta with Tart Cherry-
Cranberry Compote · page 65 ·

Pumpkin Panna Cotta with
Fresh Pomegranate Sauce · page 75 ·

Pretty in Pink Grapefruit Panna Cotta
· page 66 ·

Sweet Goat Cheese Panna Cotta
with Roasted Plums · page 77 ·

Roasted Pear Panna Cotta with Maytag
Blue Cheese · page 67 ·

Mint Julep Panna Cotta
· page 80 ·

Buttermilk Panna Cotta
with Apple Gelee · page 69 ·

Green Tea Panna Cotta
with Mirin-Lime Syrup · page 82 ·

Strawberry Daiquiri Panna Cotta
page · 89 ·

Butter Pecan Panna Cotta
· page 108 ·

Chocolate Truffle Panna Cotta
· page 100 ·

Butternut Squash Panna Cotta with
Fresh Sage and Parmesan · page 118 ·

Thai Coconut Panna Cotta
· page 103 ·

Summer Corn Panna Cotta
with Fresh Crab · page 123 ·

Ginger & Brown Sugar Panna Cotta with
Caramelized Pineapple · page 106 ·

Queso Fresco Panna Cotta with Chimichurri
& Cherry Tomatoes · page 127 ·

Panna Cotta

Also by Camilla V. Saulsbury

Cookie Dough Delights

Brownie Mix Bliss

Cake Mix Cookies

No-Bake Cookies

Puff Pastry Perfection

Panna Cotta

ITALY'S
ELEGANT
CUSTARD
MADE EASY

CAMILLA V. SAULSBURY

CUMBERLAND HOUSE
NASHVILLE, TENNESSEE

PANNA COTTA
PUBLISHED BY CUMBERLAND HOUSE PUBLISHING, INC.
431 Harding Industrial Drive
Nashville, TN 37211

Cover design: JulesRules Design
Text design: Lisa Taylor
Interior Photographs: Camilla V. Saulsbury

Library of Congress Cataloging-in-Publication Data

Saulsbury, Camilla V.
  Panna cotta : Italy's elegant custard made easy / Camilla V. Saulsbury.
    p. cm.
  Includes bibliographical references and index.
  ISBN-13: 978-1-58182-595-4 (hardcover)
  ISBN-10: 1-58182-595-1 (hardcover)
  1. Cookery (Puddings) 2. Desserts--Italy. 3. Cookery, Italian. I. Title.
  TX773.S31755 2007
  641.8'644—dc22

2007000994

Printed in Canada
1 2 3 4 5 6 7 — 12 11 10 09 08 07

To Niek

CONTENTS

ACKNOWLEDGMENTS

During the time this book was written, I finished my Ph.D., moved from Indiana to Texas, and had my first baby.

Phew!

It was a challenge at times to keep my focus on cream and sugar, but the rewards were, quite literally, sweet. I discovered in the process, too, that panna cotta is quite possibly the best summertime dessert for sticky East Texas summers.

Throughout, the staff at Cumberland House Publishing guided me through. Special thanks to: Ron Pitkin, my publisher, who is always a voice of encouragement, calm, and reason; Tracy Ford, my publicist, for making me laugh, keeping me sane, and being my number-one cheerleader; Julia Pitkin, whose cover designs delight me time and again; and Lisa Taylor, who I continue to assert is a modern-day goddess in editor disguise.

Thanks to the two people in my life who inspired me to cook in particular and explore life in general: my mother, Charlotte, and my father, Daniel. And to Sean, Robin, Becca, Kenji, Hugh, Jean, and Ray—thanks for believing in me.

To the women at Christ Church Episcopal Church in Nacogdoches, Texas, who took my panna cotta cooking class: teaching was never more fun! Thank you so much for the recipe feedback.

Special thanks to Carole Bidnick for some gentle encouragement that made me realize my options and, hence, made this book happen.

To Kevin, my one and only.

And to baby Nick, who has changed my life forever and makes every day beautiful.

Panna Cotta

Introduction

It's time for panna cotta to get its due as a dessert classic.

An exquisitely silky custard, panna cotta is at its most basic a confluence of cream, gelatin, and sugar, and a short list of other ingredients that lend it flavor. Molded in ramekins—or more simply set and served in glassware or cups—it has both a homey provenance and refined austerity, making it an ideal partner for a wide range of sumptuous trimmings from bittersweet chocolate to balsamic strawberries to Cabernet caramel sauce.

Yet despite its luxurious texture and chic presentation, panna cotta is one of the easiest desserts to prepare: soften some gelatin, warm some cream and sugar, combine the two, and the cooking is done. It can be made up to a day ahead, too, making it as ideal for an haute cuisine supper party as for the close of a cozy weeknight meal. Come serving time, simply unmold and garnish—that's it. If the crowd is large, recipes are easily doubled or tripled; if the occasion is intimate, simply halve the recipe. Since there is no baking involved, the proportions remain equivalent.

Panna cotta is more than a dessert dream come true: it can also be a savory first course. Made from a combination of cream with vegetable purées, cheeses, or fresh herbs, these panna cotte are in a class of their own in taste, style, and presentation. And like their sweet siblings, savory panna cotte have the enticements of ease, style, and sophistication.

In the pages that follow, you will find 100 recipes celebrating panna cotta. The first five chapters offer a suite of sweets—the sixth a baker's dozen of savory options. All are centered on ease of preparation, with flavors ranging from subtle to bold and everywhere in between, with plenty of innovative interpretations as well as tried-and-true classics.

In addition, you'll also find recipes for myriad panna cotta accompaniments—sauces, gastriques, jams, syrups, fresh fruits, sugared rose petals, marrons glacés, and more—that are as delectable and simple to assemble as the panna cotte themselves. Have fun mixing and matching flavors to create desserts or first courses that truly reflect your style and taste.

I hope you'll enjoy the charms of panna cotta as much as I do and that these recipes will make their way into your dessert and first-course repertoire. With a flick of the whisk, Italy's elegant custard can be yours.

A BIT OF HISTORY

Although sources agree that panna cotta has its origins in the Piedmont region of Italy, it has an otherwise mysterious pedigree. A review of Italian cookbooks dating from the sixteenth through the mid-twentieth century reveals no mention of any dessert remotely resembling panna cotta, let alone a recipe. And as late as the 1970s, panna cotta remains absent from two prominent Italian cooking texts, namely Waverley Root's *The Food of Italy* (1971) and Marcella Hazan's *Classic Italian Cook Book* (1973).

Yet panna cotta clearly has its roots in the custard family in general, and in Italy in particular. Custard begins with the ancient Romans, who used their knowledge of the binding properties of eggs to create both delicate, sweet custards flavored with honey, nuts, and spices, as well as savory custard concoctions made from the likes of eel, fish, and vegetables.

Where panna cotta diverges from the custards of ancient Rome is in the use of gelatin instead of eggs for binding. This may also explain panna cotta's belated arrival on the custard scene, for it wasn't until 1845 that industrialist, inventor, and philanthropist Peter Cooper obtained the first patent for a gelatin dessert. It was another forty-five years before Charles Knox developed the world's first pregranulated gelatin and several decades more before gel cooking, well . . . took hold.

At some point, ready-made gelatin made its way across the Atlantic and an enlightened cook conceived panna cotta. The use of gelatin makes panna cotta a nearly foolproof custard—no eggs to be scrambled by mistake, nor any chance of overcooking, because, though panna means "cooked cream," there really is no cooking at all. Rather, the cream is merely warmed to melt the gelatin and dissolve the sugar. The best panna cotta has very little gelatin; the result is not a solid gel, but rather a softly set, fine slip of a dessert, akin to the creamiest gelato or ice cream, without the freezing.

But what makes panna cotta all the more appealing is that its flavor history is just beginning. Some of the most traditional panna cotta flavors are vanilla bean, chocolate, coffee, and lemon, but these represent the mere tip of the iceberg. That's because, much like vanilla ice cream, panna cotta is a blank slate of possibilities. It wasn't long ago that ice cream options were limited to a favorite tastes; now, a wealth of flavors exists.

Panna cotta holds the same promise. Think bittersweet, white, or milk chocolate; toffee, caramel, or honey; exotic spices, such as five-spice and cardamom; fresh fruit purées, including winter pears or summer mangoes; or perhaps aromatic spirits, from Grand

Marnier to bourbon to Irish cream. Don't be surprised if you start dreaming up your own flavor ideas.

One thing is certain: with so much potential, panna cotta has a very bright and delicious future.

THE PANNA COTTA PANTRY

Dairy Products

Dairy products are the stars in panna cotta; hence the better they are, the better the panna cotta. If possible, opt for cream, sour cream, yogurt, and buttermilk with no or few additives for the best flavor and consistency.

You'll notice that many of the recipes throughout this collection contain sour cream or yogurt in addition to cream. The reason for this is to replicate the consistency of the super-thick cream of the Piedmont region's dairy country. The addition heightens the rich mouthfeel of the panna cotta and lends a very subtle tang (avoiding a flat-flavor profile).

You'll also find panna cotta reinterpreted with a wide variety of other dairy products, including crème fraîche, buttermilk, yogurt, sour cream, cream cheese, and mascarpone cheese as the primary dairy ingredients. The results are scrumptious, and, conveniently, these variations are every bit as easy to make as traditional panna cotta.

In the "enlightened" chapter, the goal was to cut back on fat and calories without sacrificing the silky richness that characterizes a good panna cotta. To achieve these ends, a variety of reduced-fat dairy products are employed, including low-fat buttermilk, low-fat plain yogurt, reduced-fat sour cream, and canned evaporated fat-free milk. When recipes in this chapter call for sour cream, be sure to use the specified reduced-fat variety as opposed to fat-free. The former has a flavor and taste very close to regular sour cream, while the latter has a notably strange taste and gummy consistency due to a long list of additives.

Gelatin

The difference between an ethereal panna cotta and a hockey puck panna cotta depends entirely on the amount of gelatin. Firmness varies on the ratio of liquid to gelatin and temperature (warm or chilled). So take extra care when measuring the gelatin to achieve the correct gelatin balance called for in each recipe.

All of the recipes in this collection call for powdered gelatin, the most commonly available form of gelatin. It comes packaged in boxes of ¼-ounce envelopes and is also available in bulk. It's important to note that the contents in prepackaged envelopes tend to be inconsistent: they are meant to contain ¼ ounce (2½ teaspoons), but this varies significantly from one package to the next (e.g., some contain as little as 2 teaspoons, others just over 2½ teaspoons). Measuring is the best insurance.

Leaf or sheet gelatin is the same substance as powdered gelatin, just packaged and sold in a different form. It is more widely used in Europe (and shows up in more European recipes) than in the States. Four gelatin sheets equals 2½ teaspoons powdered gelatin.

To obtain the most delicate texture possible, my panna cotta recipes are set with the barest amount of gelatin to keep it fully set but still delicate. That being said, if I know that the weather is going to be hot and humid, or if I'll be unmolding and plating the panna cotte ahead of time (and I know it will sit out unrefrigerated for more than a few minutes), I sometimes add a bit more gelatin (e.g., approximately ¼ teaspoon).

All of the recipes in this collection call for softening the gelatin. This is done by sprinkling it into a cold liquid (e.g., water, liqueur, lemon juice, or some of the cream) to bloom. It is perfectly fine to give the gelatin and softening liquid a gentle stir to facilitate the softening. All of the powder should be softened before adding to the warm cream mixture. Once the gelatin is heated in the cream, check that is fully dissolved: turn over the stirring spoon or spatula and run a finger over the hot cream mixture. You should not feel or see any gelatin granules.

Flavorings

Whether it's vanilla extract, spices, herbs, spirits, fresh produce, or chocolate, use the best quality you can afford or obtain.

Spices: Freshness is especially important with whole and ground spices. The best way to determine if a spice is fresh is to open the container and smell it. If it has a strong fragrance, it is still acceptable for use. If not, toss it and make a new purchase.

Vanilla: Real vanilla extract is used in multiple recipes throughout the book, adding a sweet, fragrant flavor to panna cotta. It really is worth the expense, and a little goes a long way. To preserve its flavor and to prevent evaporation, store it in a cool, dark place, with the bottle tightly closed. It will stay fresh for about two years unopened and for one year after being opened.

Chocolate: If the recipe calls for chocolate, try to use a premium brand—the difference really shows through in panna cotta since the number of ingredients is minimal. Store the chocolate in a dry, cool place between 60° and 78°. Wrapping chocolate in moisture-proof wrap or in a zip-lock plastic bag is a good idea if the temperature is higher or the humidity is above 50 percent. Chocolate can also be stored in the refrigerator.

Pouring into Molds

Pouring the liquid panna cotta custard can be a messy job if poured directly from a regular saucepan to ramekins or glasses. To keep clean-up to a minimum, try one of these methods: (1) Prepare the panna cotta in a saucepan with a pouring lip to easily pour directly from the saucepan; (2) use a ladle to transfer the liquid to the glasses or ramekins; or (3) pour the entire batch of custard into a 32-ounce Pyrex glass measuring cup or pitcher, then pour directly into the ramekins or glasses.

Transferring to and from the Refrigerator

Delivering six to eight liquid-filled ramekins to the refrigerator can be tricky. Make it a snap by placing all of the ramekins, molds, or glasses on a baking sheet before filling them. Clear a place in the refrigerator and slide the sheet in and out with ease. For extra-easy cleanup, line the sheet with a layer of foil or plastic wrap in case of small spills.

Unmolding Panna Cotta

Unmolding is the only step to panna cotta that may cause concern; it shouldn't. Simply dip the ramekin or mold into hot water (not boiling—this will melt too much of the panna cotta). Run a sharp knife around the edge, then invert onto a dessert plate. If the panna cotta needs an extra nudge, slide the knife up one side of the ramekin. Imperfections are easily smoothed out by dipping a knife into hot water and running it around the unmolded custard. If desired, the ramekins can be sprayed with a light coating of nonstick cooking spray before filling.

Presentation Possibilities

Unmolding panna cotte is an entirely optional step. To skip it, simply pour the custard into glasses and chill until set. When ready to serve, spoon or drizzle any accompaniments directly into the glass. This is beautiful as well as easy. And glasses are but one option: use your creativity and mold the panna cotte in espresso cups, china teacups, Asian teacups, or cake molds. For a family-style presentation, mold the panna cotta in a 9- or 10-inch cake pan. Unmold and slice the panna cotta into wedges or scoop out into dishes.

Panna Cotta in Less Time

To shorten preparation time, cool the panna cotta custard quickly by pouring it into a stainless steel bowl set over ice water and stir frequently until it is very cold and just begins to set. Pour the cold custard into ramekins or glasses as the recipe directs. Not only does this method shorten the chilling and gelling time by roughly half, it also produces an especially creamy, delicate custard.

Catering to a Crowd

I am of the opinion that panna cotta is one of the best dessert options for a large dinner party or gathering (it is a particularly fine option for bridal showers and baby showers). Simply double or triple (or more) the recipe, pour into disposable plastic glasses (for easy service and clean-up), and serve. All you need is enough refrigerator space for chilling.

EQUIPMENT CHECKLIST

- ✓ ¾-cup-size molds, ramekins, or custard cups (see Appendix for list of sources)
- ✓ Lipped saucepan (for easier pouring)
- ✓ 32-ounce Pyrex measuring cup
- ✓ Ladle
- ✓ Large cookie sheet (for transferring panna cotte to the refrigerator)
- ✓ Silicone or other heat-proof rubber spatulas
- ✓ Wire whisks
- ✓ Liquid measuring cups (preferably clear glass or plastic)
- ✓ Dry measuring cups in graduated sizes ¼, ⅓, ½, and 1 cup
- ✓ Measuring spoons in graduated sizes ⅛, ¼, ½, and 1 teaspoon as well as 1 tablespoon
- ✓ Wooden spoon(s)
- ✓ Mixing bowls (at least one each of small, medium, and large sizes)
- ✓ Hot mitts or holders
- ✓ Kitchen timer
- ✓ Cutting board(s)
- ✓ Chef's knife
- ✓ Small sharp knife
- ✓ Electric blender (handheld immersion or standard blender)
- ✓ Zester
- ✓ Vegetable peeler

Chapter 1

TOP-10

PANNA COTTA

FAVORITES

Vanilla Bean Panna Cotta

WITH BALSAMIC STRAWBERRIES

If you're looking for the quintessential panna cotta recipe, this is it. Yogurt adds a rich dimension to the cream, resulting in a flavor reminiscent of the thick, slightly tangy cream used in traditional Italian panna cotta recipes. The balsamic berry topping is a traditional partner to the silken, vanilla bean custard, but other accompaniments in this collection—bittersweet chocolate sauce, dulce de leche, or roasted plums, for example—are equally divine, so pick your fancy.

Place heavy cream, sugar, and vanilla bean in heavy, medium saucepan. Bring to a simmer over medium-high heat; remove from heat. Let steep, covered, 15 minutes.

Meanwhile, place water in small bowl. Sprinkle gelatin over water. Let stand 5 minutes to soften gelatin.

Remove vanilla bean; scrape seeds from pod, stirring seeds into cream mixture (discard pod). Rewarm cream mixture 2–3 minutes until very warm but not hot. Whisk in gelatin mixture until blended and gelatin is dissolved. Whisk in yogurt until blended.

Ladle or pour mixture into 8 ¾-cup custard cups, ramekins, or small molds. Loosely cover with plastic wrap and chill 4 hours or up to overnight.

Cut around edges of each panna cotta to loosen. Set each cup in shallow bowl of hot water for 10 seconds. Immediately invert each onto a plate. Serve with the balsamic strawberries. Makes 8 servings.

2¼ cups heavy whipping cream

½ cup sugar

1 whole vanilla bean, split lengthwise

¼ cup water

2 teaspoons unflavored gelatin

1 cup plain whole-milk yogurt

1 recipe Balsamic Strawberries (see below)

BALSAMIC STRAWBERRIES

1 pint fresh strawberries, hulled and sliced

2 teaspoons sugar

½ teaspoon freshly ground black pepper

1–2 tablespoons balsamic vinegar (to taste)

In a medium bowl toss the strawberries with the sugar, pepper, and balsamic vinegar to taste. Cover and chill. Bring to room temperature 15 minutes before serving panna cotta.

Bittersweet Chocolate Panna Cotta

The reigning favorite of dessert lovers everywhere, chocolate is made magical in this creamy confection, which is balanced with just the right amount of rich cream and a final accent of sweet vanilla. It's the chocolate dessert recipe to reach for when entertaining, making a special occasion treat—or just for the sheer joy of bittersweet indulgence.

1 cup milk
2 teaspoons unflavored gelatin
¼ cup sugar
2⅓ cups heavy whipping cream, divided use
6 ounces fine-quality bittersweet chocolate (not unsweetened), finely chopped
3 tablespoons unsweetened cocoa powder (not Dutch process), sifted
1 teaspoon vanilla extract
Garnishes: softly whipped cream; bittersweet chocolate curls

Place milk in small bowl. Sprinkle gelatin over milk. Let stand 5 minutes to soften gelatin.

Meanwhile, bring the sugar and ¾ cup of the cream to simmer in heavy, medium saucepan over medium heat, stirring until sugar dissolves. Remove from heat and add the chopped chocolate and cocoa powder, whisking until melted and perfectly smooth. Return to medium-heat burner and whisk in remaining cream, heating until warm. Add gelatin mixture and vanilla and whisk until gelatin is dissolved.

Ladle or pour mixture into 8 ¾-cup custard cups, ramekins, or small molds. Loosely cover with plastic wrap and chill 4 hours or up to overnight.

Cut around edges of each panna cotta to loosen. Set each cup in shallow bowl of hot water for 10 seconds. Immediately invert each onto a plate. Garnish with dollops of softly whipped cream and bittersweet chocolate curls. Makes 8 servings.

Cook's note: To make chocolate curls, shave curls from a piece of chocolate at room temperature using a vegetable peeler.

Variation

CHOCOLATE ESPRESSO PANNA COTTA

Prepare panna cotta as directed above but add 1½–2 teaspoons of instant espresso powder to the cream mixture along with the chopped chocolate (use 2 teaspoons espresso powder if you like a pronounced coffee flavor; 1½ teaspoons for more subtle coffee flavor).

PB & J Panna Cotta

This whimsical interpretation of peanut butter and jelly is irresistible to kids of all ages. And when made with the creamiest peanut butter, freshest cream, and best berries, it's heaven.

Place water in small bowl. Sprinkle gelatin over water. Let stand 5 minutes to soften gelatin.

Meanwhile, bring the cream and brown sugar just to a simmer in a heavy, medium saucepan over moderate heat, stirring until sugar is dissolved. Add gelatin mixture and whisk until dissolved. Whisk in peanut butter, sour cream, and vanilla until mixture is blended and smooth.

Ladle or pour mixture into 8 ¾-cup custard cups, ramekins, or small molds. Loosely cover with plastic wrap and chill 4 hours or up to overnight.

Cut around edges of each panna cotta to loosen. Set each cup in shallow bowl of hot water for 10 seconds. Immediately invert each onto a plate. Serve with berry compote and garnish with peanut brittle. Makes 8 servings.

¼ cup water

1¾ teaspoons unflavored gelatin

1¼ cups heavy whipping cream

⅓ cup packed dark brown sugar

¾ cup creamy-style peanut butter (do not use old-fashioned or natural)

1⅓ cups sour cream

1½ teaspoons vanilla extract

1 recipe Berry Compote (see below)

Garnish: ½ cup chopped purchased peanut brittle

BERRY COMPOTE

1 10-ounce package frozen raspberries in syrup, thawed

1⅓ cups frozen blackberries, thawed

1 cup frozen raspberries, thawed

Purée the thawed raspberries and their syrup in processor; strain through a fine mesh sieve into medium saucepan. Boil 1 minute. Remove from heat. Add blackberries and 1 cup raspberries, stirring gently just until coated with sauce; cool completely.

Lemon-Buttermilk Panna Cotta

WITH CRUSHED RASPBERRY SAUCE

Fresh lemon and tart buttermilk combine for an exceptionally light and refreshing dessert. Together with the lush raspberry sauce, this panna cotta exemplifies the fleeting pleasures of summer flavor.

Place lemon juice in small bowl. Sprinkle gelatin over lemon juice. Let stand 5 minutes to soften gelatin.

Meanwhile, bring the cream, sugar, and lemon zest to simmer in heavy, medium saucepan over medium-high heat, stirring until sugar dissolves. Remove from heat. Add gelatin mixture and whisk until dissolved. Whisk in the buttermilk and vanilla until blended.

Ladle or pour mixture into 8 ¾-cup custard cups, ramekins, or small molds. Loosely cover with plastic wrap and chill 4 hours or up to overnight.

Cut around edges of each panna cotta to loosen. Set each cup in shallow bowl of hot water for 10 seconds. Immediately invert each onto a plate. Serve with the crushed raspberry sauce. Makes 8 servings.

¼ cup fresh lemon juice

2 teaspoons unflavored gelatin

1¼ cups heavy whipping cream

½ cup sugar

1½ teaspoons finely grated lemon zest

2 cups low-fat buttermilk

½ teaspoon vanilla extract

1 recipe Crushed Raspberry Sauce
(see below)

CRUSHED RASPBERRY SAUCE

2 cups fresh or frozen, thawed
raspberries, undrained

3 tablespoons sugar

Place raspberries and their juices in a medium bowl. Crush lightly with back of spoon. Stir in 3 tablespoons sugar.

Grand Marnier Panna Cotta

Grand Marnier, the deeply flavorful, Cognac-based orange liqueur, elevates basic panna cotta to ethereal new heights. The liqueur's subtle notes of exotic spice, vanilla, and Haitian bitter orange are highlighted by the combination of cream and sour cream, making one spectacular dessert. For a dramatic contrast of flavors, consider replacing the final drizzle of Grand Marnier with Bittersweet Chocolate Sauce (see page 37).

Place ¼ cup of the Grand Marnier in a small bowl. Sprinkle gelatin over. Let stand 5 minutes to soften gelatin.

Place heavy cream and sugar in medium saucepan. Bring to a simmer over medium-high heat, stirring until sugar is dissolved; remove from heat. Whisk in gelatin mixture until blended and gelatin is dissolved. Whisk in sour cream and orange juice until blended.

Ladle or pour mixture into 8 ¾-cup custard cups, ramekins, or small molds. Loosely cover with plastic wrap and chill 4 hours or up to overnight.

Cut around edges of each panna cotta to loosen. Set each cup in shallow bowl of hot water for 10 seconds. Immediately invert each onto a plate. To serve, drizzle each panna cotta with some of the remaining ¼ cup Grand Marnier and garnish with orange zest or orange slices. Makes 8 servings.

½ cup Grand Marnier or other orange liqueur, divided use

2 teaspoons unflavored gelatin

2⅓ cups heavy whipping cream

⅓ cup sugar

½ cup sour cream

½ cup freshly squeezed orange juice

Garnish: freshly grated orange zest or thinly sliced navel oranges (peel on)

Toasted Coconut Panna Cotta

This island-inspired coconut concoction is just the thing for warm summer days when you want to keep time spent in the kitchen to a bare minimum. A tiny scoop of tropical sorbet and a shower of toasted flaked coconut secure the flavor and feeling of tropical escape.

Place coconut rum or water in small bowl. Sprinkle gelatin over. Let stand 5 minutes to soften gelatin.

Meanwhile, bring the coconut milk, cream, and sugar to simmer in heavy, medium saucepan, stirring until sugar dissolves. Add gelatin mixture and whisk until dissolved. Whisk in the sour cream and coconut extract until smooth.

Ladle or pour mixture into 8 martini glasses. Loosely cover with plastic wrap and chill 4 hours or up to overnight.

To serve, top each panna cotta with a small scoop of sorbet and sprinkle with toasted coconut. Makes 8 servings.

¼ cup coconut rum or water

2 teaspoons unflavored gelatin

1¾ cups canned unsweetened coconut milk

1 cup heavy whipping cream

½ cup sugar

½ cup sour cream

¾ teaspoon coconut extract

1 pint mango, pineapple, or other tropical fruit sorbet

1 cup sweetened flake coconut, lightly toasted (see cook's note below)

Cook's note: Toasting coconut in traditional oven: Preheat oven to 350°F. Spread 1 cup coconut evenly on a light-colored metal baking sheet. Bake for 7–10 minutes or until lightly browned, stirring frequently.

Toasting coconut in microwave oven: Spread 1 cup of the coconut evenly in a microwaveable pie plate. Microwave on high 5 minutes or until lightly browned, stirring every 2 minutes.

Coffee Toffee Panna Cotta

Even if you're not a coffee lover, you'll likely adore this panna cotta. Dark brown sugar, pure vanilla, a hit of espresso, and the buttery crunch of English toffee—what's not to love?

Place water in small bowl. Sprinkle gelatin over water. Let stand 5 minutes to soften gelatin.

Meanwhile bring the cream and brown sugar to a simmer in a heavy, medium saucepan over medium-high heat; remove from heat. Whisk in gelatin mixture, espresso powder, and vanilla extract until blended and gelatin is dissolved. Whisk in sour cream until blended.

Ladle or pour mixture into 8 ¾-cup custard cups, ramekins, or small molds. Loosely cover with plastic wrap and chill 4 hours or up to overnight.

Just before serving, heat the butterscotch topping according to the jar directions until warm but not hot.

Cut around edges of each panna cotta to loosen. Set each cup in shallow bowl of hot water for 10 seconds. Immediately invert each onto a plate. Drizzle with butterscotch topping and sprinkle plates with toffee. Makes 8 servings.

¼ cup water
2 teaspoons unflavored gelatin
2½ cups heavy whipping cream
½ cup packed dark brown sugar
1 tablespoon instant espresso or coffee powder
1 teaspoon vanilla extract
¾ cup sour cream
¾ cup premium butterscotch ice cream topping
¾ cup coarsely chopped chocolate-covered English toffee bars (such as Skor or Heath, about 6 ounces)

Lavender Panna Cotta

WITH BLUEBERRY COULIS

Each bite of this unique custard combines the delicate, floral notes of lavender with the lush summer flavor of blueberries. After about twenty minutes of hands-on preparation and a cool stay in the icebox, you'll have a sweet taste of Provence.

Bring the cream and lavender to simmer in a heavy, medium saucepan over medium-high heat. Remove from heat and let steep, covered, 15 minutes. Strain mixture through a sieve into a medium bowl. Discard the lavender.

Meanwhile, place milk in small bowl. Sprinkle gelatin over milk. Let stand 5 minutes to soften gelatin.

Return cream mixture to saucepan and re-warm 2–3 minutes over low heat until very warm. Whisk in honey and gelatin mixture until gelatin is melted. Whisk in yogurt.

Ladle or pour mixture into 8 ¾-cup custard cups, ramekins, or small molds. Loosely cover with plastic wrap and chill 4 hours or up to overnight.

Cut around edges of each panna cotta to loosen. Set each cup in shallow bowl of hot water for 10 seconds. Immediately invert each onto a plate. Serve with coulis and garnish with additional lavender flowers, if desired. Makes 8 servings.

2¾ cups heavy whipping cream
2 tablespoons dried edible lavender flowers
¼ cup low-fat milk
2 teaspoons unflavored gelatin
½ cup honey
½ cup whole-milk yogurt
1 recipe Blueberry Coulis (see below)
Garnish: fresh or dried lavender flowers

BLUEBERRY COULIS

1½ cups fresh blueberries or frozen, thawed blueberries (do not drain)
3½ tablespoons sugar
1½ teaspoons balsamic vinegar

Blend the blueberries, sugar, and balsamic vinegar in food processor 2 minutes until very smooth. Strain mixture through a fine mesh sieve into a pitcher or large measuring cup, pressing on solids. Refrigerate until ready to serve.

Cinnamon Panna Cotta

WITH STICKY TOFFEE SAUCE

The epitome of cozy, this panna cotta is a cinnamon lover's delight. It finds inspiration from sticky toffee pudding, a wickedly delicious British dessert consisting of a light, moist cake, rich with brown sugar and lightly spiced, then topped with a decadent sticky toffee sauce.

Place cream in a heavy, medium saucepan. Sprinkle gelatin over the cream. Let stand 5 minutes to soften gelatin.

Add the brown sugar to saucepan with cream. Cook and stir over low heat until both the gelatin and brown sugar are completely dissolved (do not let mixture come to a boil). Whisk in the sour cream, vanilla, and cinnamon until well-blended and smooth.

Ladle or pour mixture into 8 ¾-cup custard cups, ramekins, or small molds. Loosely cover with plastic wrap and chill 4 hours or up to overnight.

Cut around edges of each panna cotta to loosen. Set each cup in shallow bowl of hot water for 10 seconds. Immediately invert onto a plate. Spoon the sticky toffee sauce around each panna cotta. Makes 8 servings.

2½ cups heavy whipping cream

2 teaspoons unflavored gelatin

½ cup firmly packed dark brown sugar

1 cup sour cream

1½ teaspoons vanilla extract

2 teaspoons ground cinnamon

1 recipe Sticky Toffee Sauce (see below)

STICKY TOFFEE SAUCE

2 cups plus 12 tablespoons heavy whipping cream, divided use

1⅔ cups sugar

½ cup (1 stick) unsalted butter

Pinch of salt

Combine 1 cup plus 6 tablespoons cream, sugar, and butter in heavy, large saucepan. Boil over medium-high heat until mixture thickens slightly and is deep golden, stirring constantly, about 15 minutes. Remove from heat; cool 5 minutes. Gradually whisk in salt and remaining 1 cup plus 6 tablespoons cream (the mixture will bubble vigorously). Stir over low heat until mixture is smooth. Chill. Rewarm over low heat until slightly warm before using. (Can be made 1 day ahead.) Makes about 3 cups.

Cappuccino Layered Panna Cotta

This picturesque coffee confection boasts three strata: a bottom layer of espresso cream, a top layer of vanilla cream, and a thin layer of espresso gelee sandwiched between them. Beautiful served in clear glasses, you can also make these in traditional custard cups.

Place ¼ cup water in small bowl. Sprinkle 1¾ teaspoons of the gelatin over water. Let stand 5 minutes to soften gelatin.

Bring the cream and 6 tablespoons of the sugar to a simmer in a heavy, medium saucepan over moderate heat, stirring until sugar is dissolved. Whisk in gelatin mixture and vanilla, whisking until gelatin is completely dissolved. Pour half of mixture (a scant 1½ cups) into a glass measuring cup; cover and refrigerate until ready to use. Whisk 2½ teaspoons of espresso powder into remaining mixture. Pour or ladle ¼ cup espresso panna cotta into each of 6 tall 8-ounce glasses. Loosely cover with plastic wrap and refrigerate until set, about 1 hour.

For the gelee, place ¼ cup water in small bowl. Sprinkle the remaining 1¼ teaspoons gelatin over water. Let stand 5 minutes to soften gelatin.

In a small saucepan set over high heat, bring remaining 3 tablespoons sugar, remaining 1 cup water, and remaining 2 tablespoons espresso powder just to a boil. Add to gelatin mixture, whisking to dissolve gelatin; cool to room temperature. Pour 2 tablespoons espresso gelatin into each glass. Loosely cover and refrigerate to set, about 45 minutes. Pour the remaining espresso gelatin in a small baking dish. Loosely cover and refrigerate to set.

Melt the 1½ cups of refrigerated vanilla panna cotta mixture in a microwave oven until pourable but still cold, about 15 seconds. Pour or ladle ¼ cup vanilla panna cotta into each glass. Cover and refrigerate about 2 hours to set.

To serve, spoon remaining espresso gelatin into glasses on top of each panna cotta and dust with a small dash of ground cinnamon. Makes 6 servings.

1½ cups water, divided use
3 teaspoons unflavored gelatin, divided use
2¾ cups heavy whipping cream
9 tablespoons sugar, divided use
1½ teaspoons vanilla extract
2 tablespoons plus 2½ teaspoons instant espresso powder, divided use
Garnish: about ½ teaspoon ground cinnamon

Mayan Chocolate Panna Cotta

Gianduia Panna Cotta

Rocky Road Panna Cotta

Milk Chocolate Peanut Butter Panna Cotta

Pink Peppercorn Panna Cotta

Swiss Toblerone Panna Cotta

Mocha Panna Cotta

Peppermint Twist Panna Cotta

Neapolitan Panna Cotta

White Chocolate Panna Cotta

Malted Milk Ball Panna Cotta

Cannoli Panna Cotta

Caramel-Coconut Panna Cotta

Mascarpone Panna Cotta

Muscovado Butterscotch Panna Cotta

Chestnut Caramel Panna Cotta

Molasses Panna Cotta

Chai Panna Cotta

Persian-Spiced Panna Cotta

Five-Spice & Honey Panna Cotta

Cardamom Panna Cotta

Gingerbread Spice Panna Cotta

Chapter 2

CHOCOLATE,

CARAMEL,

& SPICE

Mayan Chocolate Panna Cotta

WITH MEXICAN CREMA

Deeply flavored yet not too sweet, this luscious chocolate dessert is made by layering familiar flavors of Mexico—chiles, cinnamon, vanilla, and almond—in a bittersweet chocolate custard. A quick, homemade version of Mexican crema—a cool sour cream sauce—adds a smooth and tangy contrasting finish.

Place 2⅓ cups of the heavy cream, brown sugar, cinnamon stick, and ancho chile in medium saucepan. Bring to a simmer over medium-high heat; remove from heat. Let steep, covered, 15 minutes.

Meanwhile, place milk in small bowl. Sprinkle gelatin over milk. Let stand 5 minutes to soften gelatin.

Strain the cream mixture through a fine mesh sieve into medium bowl. Return cream mixture to saucepan.

Rewarm cream mixture 2–3 minutes until very warm but not hot. Add vanilla, almond extract, and chopped chocolate, whisking until chocolate is melted (there will be small flecks of chocolate). Remove from heat and whisk in gelatin mixture until blended and gelatin is dissolved. Using an emulsion blender, blend mixture using just three on/off turns to just fully blend mixture (do not overmix).

Ladle or pour mixture into 8 ¾-cup custard cups, ramekins, or small molds. Loosely cover with plastic wrap and chill 4 hours or up to overnight.

In a small bowl whisk the sour cream and sugar with remaining ⅓ cup heavy cream until smooth. Cut around edges of each panna cotta to loosen. Set each cup in shallow bowl of hot water for 10 seconds. Immediately invert each onto a plate. Spoon crema around each panna cotta. Makes 8 servings.

2⅔ cups heavy whipping cream, divided use
3 tablespoons packed light brown sugar
1 cinnamon stick
1 dried ancho chile with seeds, stemmed, chopped
1 cup milk
2 teaspoons unflavored gelatin
1 teaspoon vanilla extract
¼ teaspoon almond extract
6 ounces bittersweet (not unsweetened) or semisweet chocolate, chopped
½ cup sour cream
2 teaspoons sugar

Gianduia Panna Cotta

Hailing from Italy, gianduia combines the nutty crunch and flavor of hazelnuts with deep rich chocolate. The beloved flavor combination has never been better than here in silky-smooth panna cotta form. Look for the chocolate-hazelnut spread in the supermarket where peanut butter is sold (Nutella is the most popular brand) or in the international foods section.

Place ¼ cup liqueur in small bowl. Sprinkle gelatin over liqueur. Let stand 5 minutes to soften gelatin.

Bring cream and sugar just to a simmer in a heavy, medium saucepan over moderate heat, stirring until sugar is dissolved. Remove from heat and add chocolate, whisking until smooth. Add gelatin mixture and whisk until dissolved. Whisk in chocolate-hazelnut spread until mixture is blended and smooth.

Ladle or pour mixture into 8 ¾-cup custard cups, ramekins, or small molds. Loosely cover with plastic wrap and chill 4 hours or up to overnight.

Cut around edges of each panna cotta to loosen. Set each cup in shallow bowl of hot water for 10 seconds. Immediately invert each onto a plate. Drizzle each panna cotta with remaining ¼ cup hazelnut liqueur and garnish with the chopped hazelnuts. Makes 8 servings.

½ cup hazelnut liqueur (e.g., Frangelico), divided use

1¾ teaspoons unflavored gelatin

2½ cups heavy whipping cream

2 tablespoons sugar

3 1-ounce squares bittersweet or semisweet chocolate, chopped

¾ cup chocolate-hazelnut spread (e.g., Nutella)

Garnish: ½ cup chopped toasted hazelnuts

Rocky Road Panna Cotta

Here the lumpy-bumpiness of rocky road is smoothed out into a luxurious custard, complete with a lavish marshmallow sauce. A sprinkling of pecans adds just the right amount of toasty crunch.

Place the light cream in a heavy, medium saucepan. Sprinkle the gelatin over the light cream. Let stand 5 minutes to soften gelatin.

Add the brown sugar to saucepan with cream mixture. Cook and stir over low heat until both the gelatin and brown sugar are completely dissolved (do not let mixture come to a boil). Whisk in the sour cream, cocoa powder, and vanilla until well-blended and smooth.

Ladle or pour mixture into 8 ¾-cup custard cups, ramekins, or small molds. Loosely cover with plastic wrap and chill 4 hours or up to overnight.

Cut around edges of each panna cotta to loosen. Set each cup in shallow bowl of hot water for 10 seconds. Immediately invert onto a plate. Spoon the marshmallow sauce on and around each panna cotta, then sprinkle with nuts. Makes 8 servings.

2⅔ cups light cream (half and half)

2 teaspoons unflavored gelatin

½ cup firmly packed dark brown sugar

⅔ cup sour cream

½ cup unsweetened cocoa powder (not Dutch process), sifted

1 teaspoon vanilla extract

1 recipe Marshmallow Sauce (see below)

1 cup chopped pecans or walnuts, lightly toasted

MARSHMALLOW SAUCE

1½ cups jarred marshmallow creme

3 tablespoons water

In a small saucepan heat the marshmallow creme and water over moderately low heat, stirring constantly until combined well. Cool sauce. Sauce may be made 4 hours ahead and kept, covered, at room temperature.

Milk Chocolate Peanut Butter Panna Cotta

The beloved combination of peanut butter and milk chocolate takes on new personality in this elegant indulgence. Peanut butter stars in the recipe: first, in the chocolate-y custard itself, then again in the over-the-top peanut butter fudge sauce.

Place water in small bowl. Sprinkle gelatin over water. Let stand 5 minutes to soften gelatin.

Meanwhile, bring the heavy cream and brown sugar just to a simmer in a heavy, medium saucepan over moderate heat, stirring until sugar is dissolved. Add gelatin mixture and milk chocolate and whisk until dissolved. Remove from heat and whisk in peanut butter, sour cream, and vanilla until mixture is blended and smooth.

Ladle or pour mixture into 8 ¾-cup custard cups, ramekins, or small molds. Loosely cover with plastic wrap and chill 4 hours or up to overnight.

Cut around edges of each panna cotta to loosen. Set each cup in shallow bowl of hot water for 10 seconds. Immediately invert each onto a plate. Serve with Peanut Butter Fudge Sauce. Makes 8 servings.

¼ cup water
1¾ teaspoons unflavored gelatin
1⅔ cups heavy whipping cream
⅓ cup packed light brown sugar
5 ounces good-quality milk chocolate, chopped
⅔ cup creamy peanut butter (do not use old-fashioned or natural)
⅔ cup sour cream
1 teaspoon vanilla extract
1 recipe Peanut Butter Fudge Sauce (see below)

PEANUT BUTTER FUDGE SAUCE

½ cup sugar
1 cup heavy whipping cream
⅓ cup creamy peanut butter (do not use old-fashioned or natural)

In a heavy saucepan cook sugar over moderate heat, without stirring, until it begins to melt. Continue cooking sugar, stirring with a fork, until melted. Continue cooking, without stirring, swirling pan instead, until deep amber.

Remove pan from heat and add cream (stand back: the caramel will bubble and steam). Return pan to heat and simmer, stirring, until caramel is dissolved. Add peanut butter, stirring until smooth.

Cook's note: The sauce may be made up to 1 week ahead and kept in an airtight container, chilled. Warm sauce slightly before serving with the panna cotta.

Pink Peppercorn Panna Cotta

WITH BITTERSWEET CHOCOLATE SAUCE

Sweet and mild, pink peppercorns are not proper members of the pepper family. Harvested from small mastic-trees, the green berries grow in tiny clusters of white flowers that form in autumn, and become bright red before harvesting. They add a subtly peppery, slightly fruity addition to this sophisticated panna cotta, as well as a faint pink hue (which you can enhance with a drop of red food coloring). Since they are too soft to be ground in a peppermill, crack any garnishing peppercorns with a mallet or the back of a knife. The accompanying bittersweet chocolate sauce makes this one divine dessert.

Bring the heavy cream, sugar, and peppercorns to simmer in a heavy, medium saucepan, stirring until sugar dissolves. Remove from heat; let stand at room temperature, covered, 1 hour to steep flavors. Strain cream through fine mesh sieve; discard peppercorns. Return cream mixture to saucepan.

Meanwhile, place water in small bowl. Sprinkle gelatin over water. Let stand 5 minutes to soften gelatin.

Rewarm cream mixture over medium heat for 2 minutes. Whisk in gelatin mixture until dissolved. Whisk in crème fraîche and red food coloring (to tint pale pink) until well blended.

Ladle or pour mixture into 8 ¾-cup custard cups, ramekins, or small molds. Loosely cover with plastic wrap and chill 4 hours or up to overnight.

Cut around edges of each panna cotta to loosen. Set each cup in shallow bowl of hot water for 10 seconds. Immediately invert onto a plate. Spoon warm bittersweet chocolate sauce around each panna cotta and, if desired, garnish with cracked peppercorns. Makes 8 servings.

2⅔ cups heavy whipping cream
⅓ cup sugar
3 tablespoons pink peppercorns, crushed
¼ cup water
2 teaspoons unflavored gelatin
⅔ cup crème fraîche or sour cream
Optional: 1–2 drops red food coloring (to enhance the pale pink color)
Optional: 1–2 tablespoons coarsely cracked pink peppercorns
1 recipe Bittersweet Chocolate Sauce (see next page)

BITTERSWEET CHOCOLATE SAUCE

| ¾ cup whipping cream |
| 2 tablespoons dark corn syrup |
| 8 ounces bittersweet (not unsweetened) chocolate, chopped |
| 1 teaspoon vanilla extract |

Bring cream and corn syrup to simmer in medium saucepan set over medium-low heat. Remove from heat. Add chocolate; stir until melted and smooth; stir in vanilla. Let stand until slightly cooled and thickened but still slightly warm, about 15–20 minutes. (Can be made 3 days ahead. Cover and chill. Stir over low heat until just warm before serving.)

Swiss Toblerone Panna Cotta

This recipe draws inspiration from Switzerland's Toblerone chocolate, an irresistible sweet containing honey-almond nougat.

Place milk in small bowl. Sprinkle gelatin over milk. Let stand 5 minutes to soften gelatin.

Meanwhile, bring ¾ cup of the cream to simmer in heavy, medium saucepan over medium heat, stirring until very warm. Remove from heat and add the chopped chocolate, whisking until melted and perfectly smooth. Return to medium heat and whisk in honey and remaining 1¼ cups cream, heating until very warm. Add gelatin mixture, vanilla, almond extract, and salt, whisking until gelatin is dissolved. Whisk in sour cream.

Ladle or pour mixture into 8 stemmed glasses (such as wine glasses). Loosely cover with plastic wrap and chill 4 hours or up to overnight.

To serve, garnish with dollops of the honey whipped cream and sprinkle with toasted sliced almonds. Makes 8 servings.

¾ cup milk

2 teaspoons unflavored gelatin

2 cups heavy whipping cream, divided use

6 ounces semisweet chocolate, chopped

3 tablespoons honey

½ cup sour cream

1 teaspoon vanilla extract

½ teaspoon pure almond extract

Pinch of salt

1 recipe Honey Whipped Cream (see below)

Garnish: ½ cup lightly toasted sliced almonds

HONEY WHIPPED CREAM

1 cup heavy whipping cream

3 tablespoons honey

1 teaspoon vanilla extract

In a medium bowl beat cream, honey, and vanilla with electric mixer set on high speed until soft peaks form.

Mocha Panna Cotta

WITH WHITE CHOCOLATE–ESPRESSO SAUCE

Panna cotta has never been more decadent. A mocha cream custard melds with a lavish drizzle of white chocolate and espresso to create a dessert masterpiece.

Place the light cream in a heavy, medium saucepan. Sprinkle the gelatin over the light cream. Let stand 5 minutes to soften gelatin.

Add the brown sugar and espresso powder to saucepan with cream mixture. Cook and stir over low heat until both the gelatin and brown sugar are completely dissolved (do not let mixture come to a boil). Whisk in the sour cream, cocoa powder, and vanilla until well-blended and smooth.

Ladle or pour mixture into 8 ¾-cup custard cups, ramekins, or small molds. Loosely cover with plastic wrap and chill 4 hours or up to overnight.

Cut around edges of each panna cotta to loosen. Set each cup in shallow bowl of hot water for 10 seconds. Immediately invert onto a plate. Spoon cooled white chocolate espresso sauce around each panna cotta. Makes 8 servings.

3 cups light cream (half and half)

2 teaspoons unflavored gelatin

½ cup firmly packed light brown sugar

2 teaspoons instant espresso or coffee powder

½ cup sour cream

⅓ cup unsweetened cocoa powder (not Dutch process), sifted

1 teaspoon vanilla extract

WHITE CHOCOLATE ESPRESSO SAUCE

¾ cup heavy whipping cream

5 ounces white chocolate (such as Lindt), chopped

2 teaspoons instant espresso or coffee powder

⅛ teaspoon ground nutmeg

Bring cream to simmer in heavy, medium saucepan. Add white chocolate and espresso powder. Stir over low heat until smooth. Stir in nutmeg. Cool to room temperature.

Peppermint Twist Panna Cotta

WITH MILK CHOCOLATE FUDGE SAUCE

Perhaps no other flavor suggests the spirit of the winter holidays more than peppermint—but this peppermint panna cotta may fast become a year-round favorite once you try it. The refreshing and creamy panna cotta and simple-to-make milk chocolate sauce are an inspired combination.

Place water in small bowl. Sprinkle gelatin over water. Let stand 5 minutes to soften gelatin.

Bring heavy cream and sugar to simmer in heavy, medium saucepan over medium-high heat, stirring until sugar dissolves. Remove from heat. Add gelatin mixture, whisking until gelatin is dissolved. Whisk in the sour cream, peppermint extract, and vanilla extract.

Ladle or pour mixture into 8 ¾-cup custard cups, ramekins, or small molds. Loosely cover with plastic wrap and chill 4 hours or up to overnight.

Cut around edges of each panna cotta to loosen. Set each cup in shallow bowl of hot water for 10 seconds. Immediately invert onto a plate. Spoon warm milk chocolate sauce around each panna cotta and sprinkle with some crushed candies. Makes 8 servings.

¼ cup water
2 teaspoons unflavored gelatin
2⅔ cups heavy whipping cream
½ cup sugar
⅔ cup sour cream
1 teaspoon pure peppermint extract
1 teaspoon vanilla extract
1 recipe Milk Chocolate Sauce (see below)
Garnish: ½ cup coarsely crushed red-and-white-striped hard peppermint candies

MILK CHOCOLATE FUDGE SAUCE

¾ cup heavy whipping cream
8 ounces imported milk chocolate (such as Lindt), chopped
½ teaspoon vanilla extract

Bring cream just to simmer in medium saucepan over medium heat. Remove from heat. Add milk chocolate; let stand 1 minute. Whisk until chocolate is melted and smooth. Whisk in vanilla. Let stand at room temperature until sauce cools and thickens slightly, about 20 minutes. (Sauce can be made 3 days ahead. Cover and chill sauce. Rewarm sauce over low heat just until pourable before serving.)

Neapolitan Panna Cotta

This nouveau interpretation of the favorite dessert combination of chocolate, vanilla, and strawberry may prove to be the ultimate temptation for your next dessert indulgence. Layers of rich chocolate and vanilla custard are cloaked in a bright red strawberry sauce, making for a dessert as stunning as it is delicious.

Make milk chocolate panna cotta: Place 2 tablespoons water in small bowl. Sprinkle 1 teaspoon gelatin over water. Let stand 5 minutes to soften gelatin.

In a heavy, small saucepan bring 1½ cups heavy cream and 2 tablespoons sugar to a simmer over moderate heat, stirring until sugar is dissolved. Whisk in chopped chocolate, whisking until chocolate is melted. Add gelatin mixture, whisking until dissolved. Pour or ladle panna cotta mixture into 6 large martini glasses. Loosely cover with plastic wrap and chill until set, about 1 hour.

Make vanilla panna cotta: Place 2 tablespoons water in small bowl. Sprinkle 1 teaspoon gelatin over water. Let stand 5 minutes to soften gelatin.

In a heavy, small saucepan over moderate heat bring 1⅔ cups cream and 3½ tablespoons sugar to a simmer, stirring until sugar is dissolved. Whisk in 1 teaspoon vanilla and gelatin mixture until dissolved. Pour or ladle panna cotta mixture into the 6 glasses, atop the chocolate layer. Loosely cover with plastic wrap and chill about 2 hours to set.

Make strawberry sauce: Purée the strawberries and sugar in a blender or food processor. Cover and refrigerate until ready to serve.

To serve, spoon strawberry sauce into glasses on top of each panna cotta. Makes 6 servings.

MILK CHOCOLATE PANNA COTTA

2 tablespoons water
1 teaspoon unflavored gelatin
1½ cups heavy whipping cream
2 tablespoons sugar
2 1-ounce squares bittersweet or semisweet chocolate, chopped

VANILLA PANNA COTTA

2 tablespoons water
1 teaspoon unflavored gelatin
1⅔ cups heavy whipping cream
3½ tablespoons sugar
1 teaspoon vanilla extract

STRAWBERRY SAUCE

1 pint strawberries, hulled and cleaned
1–2 tablespoons sugar (as needed—depends on the sweetness of the strawberries)

White Chocolate Panna Cotta

WITH CANDIED KUMQUATS

You may have seen kumquats used as autumnal table decorations, but their beauty is far more than skin deep. Believed to be native to China, these little gems of the citrus family are in fact the only citrus fruit that can be eaten whole—skin and all. They are delicious in both sweet and savory preparations, but I'm partial to eating them in simple form, either raw, or candied, as they are here. Their unique, tart-sweet flavor works exceedingly well in contrast to white chocolate.

Place orange juice in small bowl. Sprinkle gelatin over juice. Let stand 5 minutes to soften gelatin.

Meanwhile, bring the sugar and ¾ cup of the cream to simmer in heavy, medium saucepan over medium heat, stirring until sugar dissolves. Remove from heat and add the chopped white chocolate, whisking until melted and perfectly smooth. Return to medium heat and whisk in coconut milk and remaining cream, heating until warm. Add gelatin mixture and vanilla, whisking until gelatin is dissolved.

Ladle or pour mixture into 8 ¾-cup custard cups, ramekins, or small molds. Loosely cover with plastic wrap and chill 4 hours or up to overnight.

Cut around edges of each panna cotta to loosen. Set each cup in shallow bowl of hot water for 10 seconds. Immediately invert onto a plate. Serve with candied kumquats and their syrup. Makes 8 servings.

½ cup freshly squeezed orange juice, strained

2 teaspoons unflavored gelatin

2 tablespoons sugar

1⅓ cups heavy whipping cream, divided use

6 ounces fine-quality white chocolate, finely chopped

1¼ cups canned coconut milk

1 teaspoon vanilla extract

1 recipe Candied Kumquats (see below)

CANDIED KUMQUATS

¾ cup water

¾ cup sugar

24 kumquats, sliced crosswise and seeded

Combine water and sugar in small saucepan, whisking over medium heat until sugar is dissolved. Increase heat to high, bringing syrup to a boil. Add the kumquats and return to a boil. Reduce heat to medium and simmer until fruit is tender and liquid is syrupy, about 20 minutes. Transfer to a small bowl; cool completely. Cover and chill until ready to use.

Malted Milk Ball Panna Cotta

Who wouldn't covet a candy shop—inspired panna cotta, especially one that includes a malted milk cus-
tard, decadent milk chocolate sauce, and a generous sprinkle of coarsely chopped chocolate-coated malted
milk balls? It's malted milk powder that adds the distinctive flavor to the custard. It is readily available in
most supermarkets; look for it in the section where chocolate milk powder or powdered milk is shelved.

Place the light cream in a heavy, medium saucepan. Sprinkle gelatin over the cream. Let stand 5 minutes to soften gelatin.

Add the brown sugar and malted milk powder to saucepan with cream. Cook and stir over low heat until both the gelatin and brown sugar are completely dissolved (do not let mixture come to a boil). Whisk in the vanilla until well-blended and smooth.

Ladle or pour mixture into 8 ¾-cup custard cups, ramekins, or small molds. Loosely cover with plastic wrap and chill 4 hours or up to overnight.

Cut around edges of each panna cotta to loosen. Set each cup in shallow bowl of hot water for 10 seconds. Immediately invert each onto a plate. Spoon the milk chocolate sauce around each panna cotta and sprinkle with chopped malted milk balls. Makes 8 servings.

3½ cups light cream (half and half)

2 teaspoons unflavored gelatin

½ cup firmly packed light brown sugar

¾ cup malted milk powder

2 teaspoons vanilla extract

1 recipe Milk Chocolate Fudge Sauce (see page 40)

1 cup malted milk balls, coarsely chopped

Cannoli Panna Cotta

This rich and creamy confection draws its inspiration from classic Italian cannoli: shaped pastry shells that have been deep-fried, then filled with a sweetened filling of ricotta cheese, bits of chocolate, candied citron, and nuts.

Place ricotta cheese and ½ cup of the heavy cream in blender or food processor container. Cover and blend 1–2 minutes until very smooth. Set aside momentarily.

In a heavy, small saucepan, sprinkle gelatin over the remaining 1½ cups heavy cream. Let stand 5 minutes to soften gelatin. Cook and stir over low heat until the gelatin is completely dissolved (do not let mixture come to a boil). Whisk in the vanilla, almond extract, orange zest, powdered sugar and ricotta cheese mixture until blended and smooth.

Ladle or pour mixture into 8 ¾-cup custard cups, ramekins, or small molds. Loosely cover with plastic wrap and chill 4 hours or up to overnight.

Cut around edges of each panna cotta to loosen. Set each cup in shallow bowl of hot water for 10 seconds. Immediately invert each onto a plate. Spoon chocolate syrup around each panna cotta and sprinkle with pistachios and crushed cookies or pizzelles. Makes 8 servings.

1½ cups whole-milk ricotta cheese

2 cups heavy whipping cream, divided use

2 teaspoons unflavored gelatin

1 teaspoon vanilla extract

½ teaspoon pure almond extract

2 teaspoons finely grated orange zest

⅔ cup powdered sugar

¾ cup chopped roasted, lightly salted pistachios

Garnish: 1 cup coarsely crushed amaretti cookies or biscotti or 8 small pizzelle cookies (crisp Italian waffle cookies)

1 recipe Dark Chocolate Syrup (see below)

DARK CHOCOLATE SYRUP

1 cup water

½ cup sugar

⅔ cup unsweetened cocoa powder, preferably Dutch-process

¼ teaspoon salt

1 teaspoon vanilla

In a medium saucepan bring water and sugar to a boil, whisking until sugar is dissolved. Whisk in cocoa powder and salt. Simmer, whisking, until slightly thickened, about 3 minutes. Remove from heat and whisk in the vanilla. Cool syrup completely (syrup will continue to thicken as it cools).

Chocolate, Caramel, & Spice

Caramel-Coconut Panna Cotta

Complementary tropical flavors and contrasting creamy and crunchy textures make this easily assembled panna cotta a heavenly escape from the ordinary.

Place rum in small bowl. Sprinkle gelatin over rum. Let stand 5 minutes to soften gelatin.

Bring coconut milk, cream, brown sugar, and ⅓ cup caramel topping to simmer in heavy, medium saucepan over medium-high heat, stirring until sugar dissolves. Remove from heat. Add gelatin mixture and whisk until dissolved. Whisk in sour cream and coconut extract until blended and smooth.

Ladle or pour mixture into 8 ¾-cup custard cups, ramekins, or small molds. Loosely cover with plastic wrap and chill 4 hours or up to overnight.

Cut around edges of each panna cotta to loosen. Set each cup in shallow bowl of hot water for 10 seconds. Immediately invert each onto a plate. Heat remaining 1 cup caramel topping in a small saucepan set over low heat or in microwave until warm but not hot. Spoon warm caramel topping around each panna cotta and sprinkle with macadamia nuts. Makes 8 servings.

¼ cup dark rum

2 teaspoons unflavored gelatin

1⅔ cups unsweetened coconut milk

¾ cup heavy whipping cream

¼ cup packed dark brown sugar

1⅓ cups premium caramel ice cream topping, divided use

¾ cup sour cream

1 teaspoon coconut-flavored extract

1 cup coarsely chopped roasted, salted macadamia nuts

Mascarpone Panna Cotta

WITH DULCE DE LECHE SAUCE

Luxurious on every level, this recipe begins with a mascarpone-enriched custard and ends with a velvety dulce de leche sauce, the South American answer to caramel bliss. This is also exquisite with a handful of fresh berries or a drizzle of bittersweet chocolate sauce.

¼ cup water
2 teaspoons unflavored gelatin
2¼ cups whipping cream
½ cup sugar
1 8-ounce container mascarpone cheese, room temperature
1 teaspoon vanilla extract
1 recipe Dulce de Leche Sauce (see below)

Place water in small bowl. Sprinkle gelatin over water. Let stand 5 minutes to soften gelatin.

Bring the cream and sugar to simmer in heavy, medium saucepan over medium-high heat, stirring until sugar dissolves. Remove from heat. Add gelatin mixture and whisk until dissolved. Whisk in the mascarpone cheese and vanilla until blended and smooth.

Ladle or pour mixture into 8 ¾-cup custard cups, ramekins, or small molds. Loosely cover with plastic wrap and chill 4 hours or up to overnight.

Cut around edges of each panna cotta to loosen. Set each cup in shallow bowl of hot water for 10 seconds. Immediately invert each onto a plate. Spoon dulce de leche sauce over or around each panna cotta. Makes 8 servings.

DULCE DE LECHE SAUCE

1 cup heavy whipping cream
1 cup firmly packed dark brown sugar
½ cup sweetened condensed milk

In a medium saucepan set over medium heat combine the whipping cream and brown sugar, cooking and stirring until sugar dissolves. Boil until mixture is reduced to 1 cup, stirring occasionally, about 5 minutes. Stir in sweetened condensed milk. (Can be made 1 day ahead. Cover and chill. Rewarm over medium-low heat just until warm and pourable.)

Muscovado Butterscotch Panna Cotta

Muscovado sugar is an extra-dark, raw brown sugar that is produced during the third crystallization of cane syrup. It has a fine-grained texture with natural molasses to provide a strong flavor and consistency similar to refined brown sugar. Be sure to select dark muscovado sugar (it is also available in light) to produce the richest butterscotch flavor here.

Place ¼ cup water in small bowl. Sprinkle gelatin over water. Let stand 5 minutes to soften gelatin.

Meanwhile, bring the cream, ½ cup muscovado sugar, and salt just to a simmer in a medium, heavy saucepan over moderate heat, stirring until sugar is dissolved. Remove from heat momentarily.

Bring remaining ½ cup water and remaining ¼ cup muscovado sugar to a boil in a 2-quart heavy saucepan over moderate heat, stirring until sugar is dissolved. Continue to cook, stirring occasionally, until thickened and reduced to about 3 tablespoons, about 5 minutes. Remove from heat and carefully add cream mixture (mixture will bubble up and steam), whisking until combined. Whisk in gelatin mixture until dissolved.

Ladle or pour mixture into 8 ¾-cup custard cups, ramekins, or small molds. Loosely cover with plastic wrap and chill 4 hours or up to overnight.

Cut around edges of each panna cotta to loosen. Set each cup in shallow bowl of hot water for 10 seconds. Immediately invert each onto a plate. Accompany with small spoonfuls of whipped cream and a sprinkle of fleur de sel flakes. Makes 8 servings.

¾ cup water, divided use
2½ teaspoons unflavored gelatin
3 cups heavy cream
¾ cup dark muscovado sugar (or firmly packed dark brown sugar), divided use
⅛ teaspoon salt
1½ teaspoons vanilla extract
Garnish: lightly sweetened, softly whipped cream and fleur de sel (sea salt) flakes

Chocolate, Caramel, & Spice

Chestnut Caramel Panna Cotta

Marron is the French word for "chestnut," and crème de marrons is a spread, of similar consistency to apple butter, available in both cans and jars. Armagnac, a distilled grape brandy from Gascony, adds to the French allure of this recipe with its heady aromas of vanilla, toffee, pepper, rose, and chocolate. If you like, garnish each panna cotta with chopped marrons glacés, which are chestnuts that have been canned or jarred in a sweet syrup.

Whisk chestnut spread, ¼ cup milk, and salt in small bowl to combine. Set aside.

Combine sugar and ⅓ cup water in heavy, medium saucepan. Stir over medium-low heat until sugar dissolves. Increase heat and boil without stirring until syrup is deep amber color, occasionally brushing down sides and swirling pan, about 12 minutes. Slowly and carefully add cream (mixture will bubble vigorously), then remaining ¼ cup milk. Stir over low heat until any hard caramel bits dissolve and mixture is smooth. Set aside for 5 minutes.

Place Armagnac in small bowl. Sprinkle gelatin over. Let stand 5 minutes to soften gelatin.

Rewarm cream mixture over medium heat until warm but not hot. Whisk gelatin mixture until dissolved. Whisk in chestnut mixture until blended.

Ladle or pour mixture into 8 ¾-cup custard cups, ramekins, or small molds. Loosely cover with plastic wrap and chill 4 hours or up to overnight.

Cut around edges of each panna cotta to loosen. Set each cup in shallow bowl of hot water for 10 seconds. Immediately invert each onto a plate. Accompany with small spoonfuls of whipped cream and chopped chestnuts. Makes 8 servings.

¾ cup canned or jarred sweetened chestnut spread (known as crème de marrons)
½ cup whole milk, divided use
Pinch of salt
½ cup sugar
⅓ cup water
1½ cups heavy whipping cream
3½ tablespoons Armagnac
1¾ teaspoons unflavored gelatin
Garnishes: lightly whipped cream, peeled roasted chestnuts, or chopped marrons glacés

Molasses Panna Cotta

If you like the deep, intense flavor of molasses, prepare to be delighted. The toasty caramel flavors of the syrup are mellowed by the cream and sour cream, resulting in a flavor profile of subtle nuances and understated sophistication.

3¼ cups heavy whipping cream, divided use

2⅛ teaspoons unflavored gelatin

½ cup dark molasses (not blackstrap)

4 tablespoons firmly packed dark brown sugar, divided use

1 teaspoon vanilla extract

1½ cups sour cream, divided use

Place 2½ cups cream in a heavy, medium saucepan. Sprinkle gelatin over. Let stand 5 minutes to soften gelatin.

Set heat under saucepan to medium and stir until gelatin dissolves, about 5 minutes (do not boil). Add molasses and 2 tablespoons brown sugar and whisk until sugar dissolves, about 2 minutes. Remove from heat and whisk in vanilla and 1 cup sour cream.

Ladle or pour mixture into 8 ¾-cup custard cups, ramekins, or small molds. Loosely cover with plastic wrap and chill 4 hours or up to overnight.

Just before serving, whip the remaining ¾ cup whipping cream and remaining 2 tablespoons brown sugar in a medium bowl with electric mixer set on high speed until soft peaks form. Whisk in remaining ½ cup sour cream.

Cut around edges of each panna cotta to loosen. Set each cup in shallow bowl of hot water for 10 seconds. Immediately invert each onto a plate. Dollop each panna cotta with some of the brown sugar whipped cream. Makes 8 servings.

Chai Panna Cotta

These silky custards have the delicate flavors of Indian chai, a black tea redolent with spices, including cinnamon, cloves, cardamom, and ginger.

Combine cream, tea, cinnamon, cardamom, cloves, and ginger in medium saucepan. Bring to a simmer. Remove from heat. Cover and let steep 20 minutes.

Pour cream mixture through fine strainer into medium bowl. Discard solids in strainer. Return cream mixture to saucepan.

Place water in small bowl. Sprinkle gelatin over water. Let stand 5 minutes to soften gelatin.

Add brown sugar and orange zest to the cream mixture. Whisk over medium heat until sugar is dissolved. Remove from heat and whisk in gelatin mixture until blended and gelatin is dissolved. Whisk in sour cream and vanilla until blended.

Ladle or pour mixture into 8 ¾-cup custard cups, ramekins, or small molds. Loosely cover with plastic wrap and chill 4 hours or up to overnight.

Cut around edges of each panna cotta to loosen. Set each cup in shallow bowl of hot water for 10 seconds. Immediately invert each onto a plate. Serve with the raspberries. Makes 8 servings.

3 cups heavy whipping cream

1 tablespoon loose English Breakfast tea or Jasmine tea

1 cinnamon stick

8 whole cardamom pods

6 whole cloves

3 ¼-inch-thick rounds of peeled fresh ginger

¼ cup water

2 teaspoons unflavored gelatin

½ cup packed light brown sugar

½ teaspoon grated orange zest

½ cup sour cream

1 teaspoon vanilla extract

2 cups fresh raspberries

Persian-Spiced Panna Cotta

WITH CANDIED ROSE PETALS

Pure poetry, this fragrant panna cotta is light and creamy with the delicate perfume of rose water and Middle Eastern spices. For the candied rose petals, be sure to select aromatic petals that have not been treated with pesticides.

Place the cream in a medium saucepan. Sprinkle gelatin over cream. Let stand 5 minutes to soften gelatin.

Add the sugar and saffron to the saucepan with the cream. Cook and stir over low heat until both the gelatin and sugar are completely dissolved (do not let mixture come to a boil). Whisk in the yogurt, rose water, cardamom, coriander, and optional food coloring until well-blended and smooth.

Ladle or pour mixture into 8 ¾-cup custard cups, ramekins, or small molds. Loosely cover with plastic wrap and chill 4 hours or up to overnight.

To make candied rose petals, whisk egg whites in small bowl until foamy. Using a pastry brush, brush rose petals on both sides with egg whites; sprinkle on both sides with sugar. Dry on nonstick rack at least 4–6 hours or overnight.

Cut around edges of each panna cotta to loosen. Set each cup in shallow bowl of hot water for 10 seconds. Immediately invert each onto a plate. Garnish with candied rose petals. Makes 8 servings.

2¾ cups heavy whipping cream

2⅛ teaspoons unflavored gelatin

½ cup sugar

Pinch of saffron threads

¾ cup whole-milk yogurt

1¼ teaspoons rose water

¼ teaspoon ground cardamom

⅛ teaspoon ground coriander

Optional: 1–2 small drops red food coloring (to tint pale pink)

2 large egg whites

½ cup sugar

Petals from 2 organic roses (about 1 cup)

Five-Spice & Honey Panna Cotta

The exotic perfume of Chinese five-spice powder transforms this panna cotta from ordinary to extraordinary. The spice mixture is typically a combination of cinnamon, cloves, fennel seed, star anise, and Szechwan peppercorns, but may also include ginger and nutmeg. A kiss of honey, mixed into and drizzled on top of the panna cotta, adds a sweet touch.

¼ cup water
2 teaspoons unflavored gelatin
2½ cups heavy whipping cream
1 cup honey, divided use
2¼ teaspoons Chinese five-spice powder
¾ cup sour cream

Place water in small bowl. Sprinkle gelatin over water. Let stand 5 minutes to soften gelatin.

Bring cream and ½ cup honey to simmer in heavy, medium saucepan over medium-high heat, stirring until mixture is well-blended. Remove from heat. Add gelatin mixture and five-spice powder, whisking until dissolved. Whisk in the sour cream.

Ladle or pour mixture into 8 ¾-cup custard cups, ramekins, or small molds. Loosely cover with plastic wrap and chill 4 hours or up to overnight.

Cut around edges of each panna cotta to loosen. Set each cup in shallow bowl of hot water for 10 seconds. Immediately invert each onto a plate. Drizzle panna cotta with remaining ½ cup honey. Makes 8 servings.

Cardamom Panna Cotta

WITH PISTACHIO-PRALINE SAUCE

Alluringly spiced and not too sweet, this panna cotta is perfected with an exotic version of praline sauce, studded with pistachios and perfumed with more cardamom and a hint of lime.

Place water in small bowl. Sprinkle gelatin over water. Let stand 5 minutes to soften gelatin.

Bring the cream and sugar to simmer in heavy, medium saucepan over medium-high heat, stirring until sugar dissolves. Remove from heat. Add gelatin mixture and whisk until dissolved. Whisk in the sour cream, vanilla, and cardamom until blended and smooth.

Ladle or pour mixture into 8 ¾-cup custard cups, ramekins, or small molds. Loosely cover with plastic wrap and chill 4 hours or up to overnight.

Cut around edges of each panna cotta to loosen. Set each cup in shallow bowl of hot water for 10 seconds. Immediately invert each onto a plate. Spoon pistachio-praline sauce over or around each panna cotta. Makes 8 servings.

¼ cup water

2 teaspoons unflavored gelatin

1¾ cups whipping cream

½ cup sugar

1½ cups sour cream

1 teaspoon vanilla extract

½ teaspoon ground cardamom

1 recipe Pistachio-Praline Sauce (see below)

PISTACHIO-PRALINE SAUCE

¼ cup (½ stick) unsalted butter

½ cup packed light brown sugar

1 cup heavy whipping cream

¼ teaspoon ground cardamom

1½ teaspoons fresh lime juice

½ teaspoon grated lime zest

⅔ cup coarsely chopped, shelled, roasted, lightly salted pistachios

Melt butter in a nonstick medium skillet set over moderate heat. Add brown sugar, cream, and cardamom to skillet and simmer, stirring occasionally, until sauce is slightly thickened, about 5 minutes. Remove from heat and stir in lime juice, lime zest, and pistachios. Cool to lukewarm.

Chocolate, Caramel, & Spice

Gingerbread Spice Panna Cotta

WITH QUICK LEMON CURD SAUCE

Inspired by all that's great about homemade gingerbread, this spiced panna cotta tastes both old-fashioned and innovative. The accompanying lemon sauce is one of my favorite quick fixes—the fresh lemon juice and zest enliven the purchased lemon curd, resulting in a sauce that tastes 100 percent homemade.

Place orange juice in small bowl. Sprinkle gelatin over juice. Let stand 5 minutes to soften gelatin.

In a medium saucepan combine the cream, molasses and brown sugar. Heat over medium heat until hot but not boiling. Add gelatin mixture and stir until gelatin is dissolved. Remove from heat. Whisk in the ginger, cinnamon, cloves, nutmeg, cardamom, sour cream, and vanilla until blended and smooth.

Ladle or pour mixture into 8 ¾-cup custard cups, ramekins, or small molds. Loosely cover with plastic wrap and chill 4 hours or up to overnight.

To serve, immerse bottom half of each ramekin or custard cup in hot water about 15 seconds. Run a clean small knife around edge to loosen. Invert each onto a plate. Spoon lemon curd sauce around each panna cotta and serve. Makes 8 servings.

¼ cup orange juice (preferably freshly squeezed)

2 teaspoons unflavored gelatin

2 cups heavy whipping cream

⅓ cup dark molasses (not blackstrap)

¼ cup packed dark brown sugar

1 teaspoon ground ginger

½ teaspoon ground cinnamon

⅛ teaspoon ground cloves

⅛ teaspoon freshly grated nutmeg

⅛ teaspoon ground cardamom

1¼ cups sour cream

1 teaspoon vanilla extract

1 recipe Quick Lemon Curd Sauce (see below)

QUICK LEMON CURD SAUCE

1 cup purchased jarred lemon curd

¼ cup freshly squeezed lemon juice

1 teaspoon freshly grated lemon zest

In a small bowl whisk the lemon curd, lemon juice, and lemon zest until blended and smooth. Cover and refrigerate until ready to use.

Chapter 3

FRUIT

PANNA COTTA

Lemon-Thyme Panna Cotta

The key to lemon panna cotta is striking just the right balance of tart citrus and smooth cream. I think I've hit it with this rendition. And it only gets better with the elusive addition of fresh thyme in the topping. For some easy variations, partner the lemon panna cotta with any number of the fruit sauces in this collection, or keep it simple with fresh berries as accompaniment.

Bring whipping cream, sugar, and lemon zest to simmer in heavy, medium saucepan over medium-high heat; remove from heat. Let steep, covered, 20 minutes.

Meanwhile, place lemon juice in small bowl. Sprinkle gelatin over juice. Let stand 5 minutes to soften gelatin.

Remove lemon zest from cream mixture with a slotted spoon. Rewarm cream 2–3 minutes over low heat until very warm. Whisk in gelatin mixture until gelatin is melted. Whisk in yogurt.

Ladle or pour mixture into 8 ¾-cup custard cups, ramekins, or small molds. Loosely cover with plastic wrap and chill 4 hours or up to overnight.

Cut around edges of each panna cotta to loosen. Set each cup in shallow bowl of hot water for 10 seconds. Immediately invert each onto a plate. Drizzle with lemon-thyme drizzle and garnish with thyme sprigs. Makes 8 servings.

2 cups heavy whipping cream
½ cup sugar
4 2 x ½-inch strips lemon zest
5 tablespoons fresh lemon juice
2 teaspoons unflavored gelatin
1¼ cups low-fat plain yogurt
1 recipe Lemon-Thyme Drizzle (see below)
Garnish: fresh thyme sprigs

LEMON-THYME DRIZZLE

½ cup honey
2 tablespoons fresh lemon juice
2½ teaspoons finely chopped fresh thyme

In a small saucepan set over low heat combine honey, lemon juice, and thyme. Bring mixture to a simmer over low heat. Stir to blend. Remove from heat and cool completely. Cover and refrigerate until ready to use.

Saffron Panna Cotta

WITH BLOOD ORANGES

Coming from the dried stigmas of the saffron crocus, it takes 75,000 blossoms or 225,000 hand-picked stigmas to make a single pound of saffron, which explains why it is the world's most expensive spice. A native of the Mediterranean, saffron is now imported primarily from Spain, where Muslims introduced it in the eighth century along with rice and sugar. Although typically used in savory dishes, the pungent bitter-honey taste is an exquisite flavor for panna cotta, particularly when partnered with vivid red, tart-sweet sections of blood orange.

Bring the cream, saffron, blood orange zest, and ½ cup honey to simmer in heavy medium saucepan over medium-high heat, stirring until hot but not boiling. Remove from heat. Cover and let steep 20 minutes.

Meanwhile, place water in small bowl. Sprinkle gelatin over water. Let stand 5 minutes to soften gelatin.

Remove orange zest from cream mixture with slotted spoon; discard. Rewarm cream mixture over medium heat for 2–3 minutes. Add gelatin mixture and whisk until dissolved. Whisk in yogurt.

Ladle or pour mixture into 8 ¾-cup custard cups, ramekins, or small molds. Loosely cover with plastic wrap and chill 4 hours or up to overnight.

In a medium bowl combine the blood orange segments, blood orange juice, and remaining tablespoon honey. Loosely cover and refrigerate until ready to serve.

Cut around edges of each panna cotta to loosen. Set each cup in shallow bowl of hot water for 10 seconds. Immediately invert each onto a plate. Divide blood orange mixture among panna cotta. Makes 8 servings.

2½ cups heavy whipping cream

¾ teaspoon saffron threads

4 2x½-inch strips blood orange zest

½ cup plus 1 tablespoon honey, divided use

¼ cup water

2 teaspoons unflavored gelatin

¾ cup whole-milk yogurt

3 blood oranges, peeled, pith removed, and cut into segments

¼ cup-fresh squeezed blood orange juice (from about 1 blood orange)

Lime & White Chocolate Panna Cotta

WITH STRAWBERRIES & KIWI

Even if you typically insist on your chocolate being bittersweet, you will (without question) swoon over this white chocolate treat. The tart tang of lime is an ideal partner to the sweet, smooth chocolate; the fresh fruit is a fitting crown of summer flavor.

⅓ cup fresh lime juice

2 teaspoons unflavored gelatin

3 tablespoons sugar

1 teaspoon finely grated lime zest

2 cups heavy whipping cream, divided use

6 ounces fine-quality white chocolate, finely chopped

1 cup sour cream

1 teaspoon vanilla extract

2 cups sliced hulled strawberries

2 kiwi fruit, peeled, halved lengthwise, and thinly sliced

Place lime juice in small bowl. Sprinkle gelatin over juice. Let stand 5 minutes to soften gelatin.

Meanwhile, bring the sugar, lime zest, and ¾ cup of the cream to simmer in heavy, medium saucepan over medium heat, stirring until sugar dissolves. Remove from heat and add the chopped white chocolate, whisking until melted and perfectly smooth. Return to medium heat and whisk in remaining 1¼ cups cream, heating until warm. Add gelatin mixture, whisking until gelatin is dissolved. Whisk in sour cream and vanilla.

Ladle or pour mixture into 8 ¾-cup custard cups, ramekins, or small molds. Loosely cover with plastic wrap and chill 4 hours or up to overnight.

Cut around edges of each panna cotta to loosen. Set each cup in shallow bowl of hot water for 10 seconds. Immediately invert onto a plate. Serve with the strawberries and kiwi. Makes 8 servings.

Raspberry Panna Cotta

Sheer raspberry heaven, this luscious summer treat has a triple hit of raspberry: fresh raspberries and raspberry preserves in the custard and a generous helping of fresh raspberry compote spooned over all.

Place the raspberries and buttermilk in a blender or food processor; purée until very smooth, then pour through a fine-mesh sieve into a bowl, pressing on and then discarding solids. (Mixture should measure 2¼ cups total. Add more buttermilk if needed).

Place water in small bowl. Sprinkle gelatin over water. Let stand 5 minutes to soften gelatin.

While gelatin softens, heat cream and preserves in a medium saucepan set over moderate heat until hot, stirring until preserves are melted and mixture is well-blended. Remove from heat and whisk in gelatin mixture, whisking until gelatin is dissolved. Whisk cream mixture into raspberry purée until blended.

Ladle or pour mixture into 6 ¾-cup custard cups, ramekins, or small molds. Loosely cover with plastic wrap and chill 4 hours or up to overnight.

Cut around edges of each panna cotta to loosen. Set each cup in shallow bowl of hot water for 10 seconds. Immediately invert each onto a plate. Spoon the compote over and around each panna cotta. Makes 6 servings.

3 cups fresh or unsweetened frozen, thawed (undrained) raspberries

1 cup buttermilk

¼ cup water

2¼ teaspoons unflavored gelatin

½ cup heavy whipping cream

⅔ cup seedless raspberry preserves or jam

1 recipe Raspberry Compote (see below)

RASPBERRY COMPOTE

2 cups fresh or unsweetened frozen, thawed raspberries

½ cup seedless raspberry preserves or jam

¼ cup water

2 tablespoons fresh lemon juice

Place the raspberries in a medium bowl. In a small saucepan whisk the preserves and water until blended. Bring to a boil over moderate heat, stirring occasionally. Stir in lemon juice, then pour syrup over raspberries and gently stir to combine.

Peaches & Cream Panna Cotta

Here's a dessert that combines the ideals of urban sophistication with country charm. If fresh peaches are out of season, an equal amount of frozen, thawed peaches may be substituted.

Place the peaches in a blender or food processor. Purée until very smooth. Measure 1½ cups peach purée into 2-cup glass measuring cup; set aside. Cover and chill remaining peach purée for final presentation.

Place the cream in a medium saucepan. Sprinkle the gelatin over. Let stand 5 minutes to soften gelatin. Add the sugar to saucepan and bring to simmer over medium-high heat, stirring until sugar and gelatin are dissolved. Remove from heat. Whisk in the 1½ cups peach purée, sour cream, and lemon juice until blended and smooth.

Ladle or pour mixture into 8 ¾-cup custard cups, ramekins, or small molds. Loosely cover with plastic wrap and chill 4 hours or up to overnight.

Cut around edges of each panna cotta to loosen. Set each cup in shallow bowl of hot water for 10 seconds. Immediately invert each onto a plate. Spoon the reserved peach purée around each panna cotta. Makes 8 servings.

4 cups peeled, pitted, and sliced peaches (about 2 pounds) or 4 cups frozen, thawed sliced peaches

1½ cups heavy whipping cream

2 teaspoons unflavored gelatin

⅓ cup sugar

½ cup sour cream

2 tablespoons fresh lemon juice

Fruit Panna Cotta

New York Cheesecake Panna Cotta

WITH MARMALADE-LEMON GLAZE

Some dessert icons, such as New York–style cheesecake, are so exceptional that they qualify for all sorts of new interpretations. Embellished with a two-step, two-ingredient orange and lemon glaze, this inspired panna cotta will thrill dessert lovers everywhere.

Combine water and lemon juice in small bowl. Sprinkle gelatin over. Let stand 5 minutes to soften gelatin.

In a medium saucepan combine the cream and sugar. Cook and stir over medium heat until sugar is dissolved. Add gelatin mixture and stir until gelatin is dissolved. Remove from heat. Whisk in the softened cream cheese, continuing to whisk until melted and smooth. Whisk in sour cream and vanilla until smooth and blended.

Ladle or pour mixture into 8 ¾-cup custard cups, ramekins, or small molds. Loosely cover with plastic wrap and chill 4 hours or up to overnight.

Cut around edges of each panna cotta to loosen. Set each cup in shallow bowl of hot water for 10 seconds. Immediately invert each onto a plate. Spoon the marmalade-lemon glaze over each panna cotta and, if desired, garnish with mint sprigs. Makes 8 servings.

2 tablespoons water
2 tablespoons fresh lemon juice
1¾ teaspoons unflavored gelatin
1¾ cups heavy whipping cream
½ cup sugar
1 8-ounce package cream cheese, cut into small pieces, softened
½ cup sour cream
1½ teaspoons vanilla extract
1 recipe Marmalade-Lemon Glaze (see below)
Garnish: fresh mint sprigs

MARMALADE-LEMON GLAZE

1 cup orange marmalade
3 tablespoons fresh lemon juice

Combine the orange marmalade and lemon juice in a small saucepan set over low heat, stirring until marmalade is melted and mixture is blended. Cool to room temperature before using with panna cotta.

Striped Red Fruit Panna Cotta Parfaits

Refreshing without being heavy, the striped effect of this panna cotta is beautiful, and the tanginess of the fruit cuts the richness of the dairy. The result is an irresistible dessert—for Christmas or Valentine's Day, in particular—you won't soon forget.

Place ¼ cup of the juice in a small bowl; sprinkle with 1½ teaspoons of the gelatin. Let stand 5 minutes to soften.

Meanwhile, bring the remaining juice to a boil in heavy, medium saucepan over high heat; boil until reduced by half (1½ cups). Add gelatin mixture and whisk until gelatin is dissolved. Let cool 15 minutes. Reserve ¾ cup of the mixture. Ladle or pour the remaining mixture into 6 Champagne flutes. Refrigerate the flutes until the gelatin is chilled and set, at least 2 hours.

Place cream in a heavy, medium saucepan. Sprinkle the remaining 1¼ teaspoons gelatin over the cream. Let stand 5 minutes to soften gelatin. Add sugar to saucepan with cream. Cook and stir over low heat until both the gelatin and sugar are completely dissolved (do not let mixture come to a boil). Whisk in the crème fraîche and lemon extract until well-blended and smooth. Let cool 30 minutes.

Carefully ladle or pour the crème fraîche panna cotta into the Champagne flutes and chill until set, about 2 hours. Rewarm the remaining red juice gelatin over low heat until it's just pourable; pour a thin layer over the panna cotta in each flute. Refrigerate until set, about 30 minutes. Serve the parfaits with the fruit and toasted nuts. Makes 6 servings.

3¼ cups pomegranate, cherry or cranberry juice, divided use

2¾ teaspoons unflavored gelatin, divided use

1¼ cups heavy whipping cream

3 tablespoons sugar

1 cup crème fraîche or sour cream

½ teaspoon pure lemon extract

Garnish: fresh pitted cherries, halved, or pomegranate seeds; coarsely chopped toasted walnuts

Yogurt Panna Cotta

WITH POACHED APRICOTS

Light and silky, this well-dressed dessert is an ideal choice for intimate dinner parties or entertaining a crowd. In either case, the combination of tangy-sweet panna cotta and succulent apricots will guarantee love at first bite.

Place water in small bowl. Sprinkle gelatin over water. Let stand 5 minutes to soften gelatin.

Bring the cream and sugar to simmer in heavy, medium saucepan over medium-high heat, stirring until sugar dissolves. Remove from heat. Add gelatin mixture and whisk until dissolved. Whisk in the yogurt and vanilla until blended.

Ladle or pour mixture into 8 ¾-cup custard cups, ramekins, or small molds. Loosely cover with plastic wrap and chill 4 hours or up to overnight.

Cut around edges of each panna cotta to loosen. Set each cup in shallow bowl of hot water for 10 seconds. Immediately invert each onto a plate. Serve with poached apricots. Makes 8 servings.

¼ cup water
2 teaspoons unflavored gelatin
1¼ cups heavy whipping cream
½ cup sugar
2 cups plain whole-milk or low-fat yogurt
1 teaspoon vanilla extract
1 recipe Poached Apricots (see next column)

POACHED APRICOTS

1 cup water
3 tablespoons honey
3 tablespoons sugar
1 pound fresh apricots, pitted and quartered
½ teaspoon vanilla extract

In a medium saucepan simmer the water, honey, and sugar, covered, for 5 minutes. Add the apricots and simmer, covered, until just tender but not falling apart, about 4–5 minutes (depending on the ripeness of the fruit). Transfer apricots with a slotted spoon to a bowl and boil syrup until reduced to about ½ cup. Stir the vanilla into the syrup. Pour syrup over apricots and chill until ready to serve.

Cook's note: Canned, drained apricot halves (approximately 1½ 15-ounce cans) may be substituted for fresh apricots. Reduce apricot cook time to 2–3 minutes.

Maple Panna Cotta

WITH TART CHERRY-CRANBERRY COMPOTE

Accented with a tart, red compote, this panna cotta recipe is a heavenly marriage of fall flavors. Although any pure maple syrup will work here, Grade B maple syrup is preferable: it is darker and more assertively flavored, leading to panna cotta with an especially deep maple flavor.

Place cream in medium saucepan. Sprinkle gelatin over cream. Let stand 5 minutes to soften gelatin.

Set heat under saucepan to medium and stir until gelatin dissolves, about 5 minutes (do not boil). Add brown sugar, maple syrup, and salt and whisk until sugar dissolves, about 2 minutes. Remove from heat and whisk in buttermilk and maple extract.

Ladle or pour mixture into 8 ¾-cup custard cups, ramekins, or small molds. Loosely cover with plastic wrap and chill 4 hours or up to overnight.

Cut around edges of each panna cotta to loosen. Set each cup in shallow bowl of hot water for 10 seconds. Immediately invert each onto a plate. Spoon the tart cherry-cranberry sauce around each panna cotta. Makes 8 servings.

2½ cups heavy whipping cream

2 teaspoons unflavored gelatin

2 tablespoons firmly packed dark brown sugar

½ cup pure maple syrup (preferably Grade B)

⅛ teaspoon salt

1 cup buttermilk

1 teaspoon maple-flavored extract

1 recipe Tart Cherry-Cranberry Compote (see below)

TART CHERRY-CRANBERRY COMPOTE

1½ cups cranberry juice cocktail

¾ cup dried tart cherries

⅓ cup sugar

1 cup (half of a 12-ounce package) fresh cranberries

¼ teaspoon ground cinnamon

In a heavy, medium saucepan set over medium heat bring the cranberry juice to a simmer. Remove from heat. Add cherries and let stand 8 minutes. Mix in sugar, then cranberries and cinnamon. Cook over medium-high heat until cranberries burst, stirring occasionally, about 9 minutes. Refrigerate until cold, about 4 hours (sauce will thicken as it cools).

Pretty in Pink Grapefruit Panna Cotta

Grapefruit may seem an unusual combination with cream, but the two coalesce into a silky smooth masterpiece. The bittersweet flavor and pale pink hue of grapefruit are further enhanced with the addition of Campari, the bright red Italian aperitif. Select regular, as opposed to sweet, Campari for a bittersweet flavor. And if you don't wish to fuss with peeling and removing the pith of the accompanying grapefruit sections, look for peeled pink grapefruit sections, packed in light syrup, in the produce section of the supermarket.

Pour 4 tablespoons Campari in a small bowl. Sprinkle gelatin over. Let stand 5 minutes to soften gelatin.

Bring grapefruit juice and ½ cup sugar to simmer in heavy medium saucepan over medium-high heat, stirring until sugar dissolves. Remove from heat. Add gelatin mixture and whisk until dissolved. Whisk whipping cream into grapefruit mixture until blended. If mixture is not sufficiently pale pink, add 1-2 drops red food coloring, if desired.

Ladle or pour mixture into 8 ¾-cup custard cups, ramekins, or small molds. Loosely cover with plastic wrap and chill 4 hours or up to overnight.

In a medium bowl combine grapefruit segments and their juices, remaining 2 tablespoons Campari, and remaining tablespoon sugar. Refrigerate until ready to serve panna cotta.

Cut around edges of each panna cotta to loosen. Set each cup in shallow bowl of hot water for 10 seconds. Immediately invert each onto a plate. Divide grapefruit segments and Campari liquid among plates. Makes 8 servings.

6 tablespoons Campari, divided use (or use additional grapefruit juice)

2¼ teaspoons unflavored gelatin

1½ cups strained fresh ruby-red grapefruit juice

⅓ cup plus 1 tablespoon sugar, divided use

1¾ cups heavy whipping cream

Optional: 1–2 drops red food coloring

3 medium-size pink grapefruits, peel & pith removed, cut into sections, juices reserved

Roasted Pear Panna Cotta

WITH MAYTAG BLUE CHEESE

A kaleidoscope of autumn flavors, this panna cotta is as simple as it is delicious.

Strain pear nectar through a fine mesh sieve over a small bowl; discard solids. Sprinkle gelatin over strained nectar. Let stand 5 minutes to soften gelatin.

Place cream and sugar in a medium saucepan; stir in nectar-gelatin mixture. Cook over medium-low heat until gelatin dissolves, stirring constantly. Set heat under saucepan to medium and continue to stir for about 5 minutes (do not boil). Remove from heat and whisk in the lemon juice and nutmeg.

Ladle or pour mixture into 8 ¾-cup custard cups, ramekins, or small molds. Loosely cover with plastic wrap and chill 4 hours or up to overnight.

Cut around edges of each panna cotta to loosen. Set each cup in shallow bowl of hot water for 10 seconds. Immediately invert each onto a plate. Divide the roasted pears around each panna cotta. Sprinkle each serving with 2 tablespoons cheese. Makes 8 servings.

2 cups pear nectar

2¼ teaspoons unflavored gelatin

1½ cups heavy whipping cream

3 tablespoons sugar

1 tablespoon fresh lemon juice

⅛ teaspoon ground nutmeg

1 recipe Roasted Pears (see below)

1 cup (4 ounces) crumbled Maytag or other blue cheese

ROASTED PEARS

4 firm-ripe Bartlett pears (about 2½ pounds), peeled, halved, and cored

¼ cup honey

¼ teaspoon salt

Preheat oven to 400°F. Cut pears into ½-inch-wide slices. Place pears on rimmed baking sheet and drizzle with honey; sprinkle with salt. Bake until pears are tender, about 15 minutes. Cool completely on baking sheet.

Fruit Panna Cotta

Panna Cotta

WITH BLACKBERRY COMPOTE & FRESH SAGE

The pungent, musty-mint aroma of sage, more typically associated with savory dishes, is the subtle, enchanting flavor note in this sophisticated panna cotta. The blackberry compote is a snap to prepare and makes a splendid complement.

Bring cream, sugar, and chopped sage to simmer in heavy, medium saucepan over medium-high heat, stirring until sugar dissolves. Remove from heat. Cover and let steep 20 minutes.

Place water in small bowl. Sprinkle gelatin over water. Let stand 5 minutes to soften gelatin.

Strain the cream mixture through a fine mesh sieve into a medium bowl, pressing on solids. Discard sage. Return cream mixture to saucepan. Rewarm over medium heat until very warm. Remove from heat and add gelatin mixture, whisking until dissolved. Whisk in yogurt and vanilla.

Ladle or pour mixture into 8 ¾-cup custard cups, ramekins, or small molds. Loosely cover with plastic wrap and chill 4 hours or up to overnight.

Cut around edges of each panna cotta to loosen. Set each cup in shallow bowl of hot water for 10 seconds. Immediately invert onto a plate. Serve with blueberry compote and garnish with sage leaves. Makes 8 servings.

2½ cups heavy whipping cream

½ cup sugar

⅓ cup coarsely chopped fresh sage

¼ cup water

2 teaspoons unflavored gelatin

¾ cup plain whole-milk yogurt

1 teaspoon pure vanilla extract

1 recipe Blackberry Compote (see below)

Garnish: fresh sage leaves

BLACKBERRY COMPOTE

2 cups fresh or frozen, thawed blackberries (do not drain)

⅓ cup sugar

2 tablespoons fresh lemon juice

Place the blackberries, sugar, and lemon juice in medium bowl; gently toss to combine. Let stand until sugar dissolves and juices form, stirring occasionally, about 1 hour. (The compote can be made up to 2 days ahead. Cover and refrigerate until ready to serve.)

Buttermilk Panna Cotta

WITH APPLE GELEE

The buttermilk of days past was the liquid that remained after butter was churned. These days it gets it distinctive taste and texture from the addition of a special bacteria to low-fat or nonfat milk. It is a fine ingredient for panna cotta, producing a light, tangy custard that is immensely satisfying, especially when partnered with the vibrant flavors of fresh Fuji apples.

In a medium saucepan sprinkle 1½ teaspoons gelatin over the heavy cream in medium saucepan (do not stir). Let stand 5 minutes to soften gelatin. Add ½ cup of the sugar. Cook and stir over low heat until both the gelatin and sugar are completely dissolved (do not let mixture come to a boil). Whisk in the buttermilk until well-blended and smooth.

Ladle or pour mixture into 6 martini glasses or other decorative glasses. Loosely cover with plastic wrap and chill 3 hours or up to overnight.

After the panna cotta has set for at least 2 hours, make the gelee. Place 2 tablespoons lemon juice in a small bowl. Sprinkle the remaining 1¼ teaspoons gelatin over the juice and let stand to soften, about 5 minutes. Bring the apple juice and 3 tablespoons of the remaining sugar to a boil in a small pan over high heat. Pour hot apple mixture over the gelatin mixture; whisk to dissolve. Let cool to room temperature.

Once the buttermilk panna cotta has set, pour a ¼-inch-thick layer of apple gelee on top of each dessert. Refrigerate until firm, at least 30 minutes.

In a small bowl toss the diced apples with the remaining tablespoon sugar and remaining tablespoon lemon juice. Loosely cover and refrigerate until ready to serve.

Serve chilled, topped with the diced apples in each glass. Makes 6 servings.

2¾ teaspoons unflavored gelatin, divided use

⅔ cup whipping cream

¾ cup sugar, divided use

2 cups buttermilk

3 tablespoons fresh lemon juice, divided use

1⅓ cups filtered, unsweetened apple juice

2 medium Fuji apples, unpeeled, cut into ¼-inch dice

Fruit Panna Cotta

Whipped Cream Panna Cotta

WITH CHERRY, PORT, & STAR ANISE GLAZE

The combination of cherries, fine port, and star anise coalesce into a show-stopping partner to this extra-silky panna cotta, which gets its ethereal texture by folding whipped heavy cream into the custard. Star anise is a brown, star-shaped seedpod that can be found at Asian markets and specialty foods stores, as well as in the spice section of some supermarkets. If star anise is unavailable, a cinnamon stick makes a fine substitution.

Place milk in small bowl. Sprinkle gelatin over milk. Let stand 5 minutes to soften gelatin.

In a large saucepan whisk together 1 cup cream, powdered sugar, and salt. Bring to simmer over medium heat, stirring occasionally. Remove pan from heat and add gelatin mixture, whisking until gelatin is dissolved. Whisk in sour cream and vanilla. Pour mixture into a large metal bowl and chill, stirring occasionally, until cooled to room temperature, about 15 minutes.

In a chilled bowl, beat remaining ¾ cup cream until it just holds stiff peaks. Gently fold whipped cream into cooled gelatin mixture until smooth.

Ladle or pour mixture into 8 ¾-cup custard cups, ramekins, or small molds. Loosely cover with plastic wrap and chill 4 hours or up to overnight.

Cut around edges of each panna cotta to loosen. Set each cup in shallow bowl of hot water for 10 seconds. Immediately invert each onto a plate. Serve with cherry, port, and star anise glaze. Makes 8 servings.

¼ cup milk

2⅛ teaspoons unflavored gelatin

1¾ cups heavy whipping cream, divided use

¾ cup powdered sugar

⅛ teaspoon salt

1 cup sour cream

1 teaspoon pure vanilla extract

1 recipe Cherry, Port & Star Anise Glaze (see below)

CHERRY, PORT & STAR ANISE GLAZE

2 cups stemmed, pitted tart cherries or 2 cups canned, drained tart cherries

¾ cup ruby port

½ cup sugar

2 tablespoons balsamic vinegar

3 whole star anise

1 whole cinnamon stick

Stir cherries, port, sugar, and vinegar in heavy, large skillet over high heat until sugar dissolves.

Bring to boil; reduce heat to medium and simmer until cherries are soft and wooden spoon leaves path in sauce when drawn across bottom of skillet, about 15 minutes. Remove from heat and remove star anise and cinnamon stick with slotted spoon. Cool to room temperature. (Can be made 2 days ahead. Cover and refrigerate. Bring to room temperature before continuing.)

Fruit Panna Cotta

Hachiya Persimmon Panna Cotta

The secret to success with this elegant, autumnal dessert is choosing very ripe Hachiya persimmons—less than ripe ones are highly tannic and astringent. A ripe persimmon has considerable give when squeezed (akin to a water balloon) and will have a somewhat translucent appearance.

Purée persimmons in a food processor until smooth. Strain purée through a mesh sieve. (Should yield approximately 2½ cups of persimmon purée.)

Combine water and lemon juice in small bowl. Sprinkle gelatin over. Let stand 5 minutes to soften gelatin.

Bring the cream, sugar, and salt to simmer in heavy, medium saucepan over medium-high heat, stirring until sugar dissolves. Remove from heat. Add gelatin mixture and whisk until dissolved. Add the cardamom and 1¾ cups of the persimmon purée, whisking until combined. Place the remaining purée in a small bowl; cover surface with a round of wax paper, then cover bowl with plastic wrap and refrigerate.

Ladle or pour mixture into 8 ¾-cup custard cups, ramekins, or small molds. Loosely cover with plastic wrap and chill 4 hours or up to overnight.

Cut around edges of each panna cotta to loosen. Set each cup in shallow bowl of hot water for 10 seconds. Immediately invert each onto a plate. Serve with a dollop of whipped cream and a drizzle of some of the reserved 1 cup persimmon purée. Makes 8 servings.

2½ pounds very ripe Hachiya persimmons, calyxes removed, quartered

2 tablespoons water

2 tablespoons fresh lemon juice

2 teaspoons unflavored gelatin

1⅔ cups heavy whipping cream

3 tablespoons sugar

⅛ teaspoon salt

¼ teaspoon ground cardamom

Garnish: lightly sweetened, lightly whipped cream

Cook's note: The persimmon purée may be prepared up to 3 days in advance of preparing the panna cotta. (Cover and chill in refrigerator.)

Sweet Anise Panna Cotta

WITH RHUBARB JAM

The greenish-brown, oval seeds of the anise plant have a sweet licorice flavor that has been used to flavor perfumes and confections since ancient times. Here its distinctive flavor is used to flavor panna cotta, with immensely satisfying results. As a tart-sweet accompaniment, cherry-red stalks of rhubarb are simmered to a jam-like consistency, then spooned alongside each custard. For convenience, or if rhubarb is out of season, look for bags of frozen rhubarb—typically cut into chunks—in the frozen fruit section of your grocer's freezer.

Bring cream, sugar, and anise seeds to simmer in heavy, medium saucepan, stirring until sugar dissolves. Remove from heat; let stand at room temperature, covered, 1 hour to steep flavors. Strain cream through fine mesh sieve; discard anise seeds. Return cream mixture to saucepan.

Place water in small bowl. Sprinkle gelatin over water. Let stand 5 minutes to soften gelatin.

Rewarm cream mixture over medium heat for 2–3 minutes until very warm. Whisk in gelatin mixture until dissolved. Whisk in sour cream until well blended.

Ladle or pour mixture into 8 low, clear bar glasses or other low, decorative glasses. Loosely cover with plastic wrap and chill 4 hours or up to overnight.

Spoon rhubarb jam atop each panna cotta just before serving. Makes 8 servings.

2⅓ cups heavy whipping cream
½ cup sugar
3 tablespoons anise seed
¼ cup water
2 teaspoons unflavored gelatin
1 cup sour cream
1 recipe Rhubarb Jam (see below)

RHUBARB JAM

⅔ cup sugar
2 cups fresh or frozen, thawed sliced rhubarb
1 tablespoon fresh lemon juice
¼ teaspoon pure vanilla extract
3–4 drops red food coloring

Combine sugar, rhubarb, and lemon juice in heavy, medium saucepan. Stir over medium heat until sugar dissolves. Reduce heat to medium low, cover, and simmer until rhubarb is tender, breaking up with a spoon. Transfer to bowl and stir in vanilla and enough food coloring to tint dark pink. Chill until cold, about 2 hours.

Fruit Panna Cotta

Mango Panna Cotta

WITH JASMINE TEA SYRUP

East meets West in this exotic panna cotta, whose custard is made with luscious mangoes, lime juice and ginger, and then drizzled with a mellow, jasmine-scented syrup. Fresh mangoes are preferable, but to save time, frozen (thawed) mango chunks may be substituted.

2½ cups diced firm-ripe mangoes (about 5 medium mangoes)

1¾ cups heavy whipping cream, divided use

¼ cup fresh lime juice

2½ teaspoons unflavored gelatin

⅓ cup sugar

¾ teaspoon ground ginger

1 recipe Jasmine Tea Syrup (see below)

Garnish: fresh tropical flowers or fresh mint sprigs

Place the mangoes and ½ cup of the cream in a blender or food processor; purée until very smooth, then pour through a fine-mesh sieve into a bowl, pressing on and then discarding solids. (This should yield about 2 cups of purée.)

Place lime juice in small bowl. Sprinkle gelatin over lime juice. Let stand 5 minutes to soften gelatin.

While gelatin softens, heat sugar and remaining cream in a medium saucepan set over moderate heat until hot, stirring until sugar is dissolved. Remove from heat and whisk in gelatin mixture, whisking until gelatin is dissolved. Whisk cream mixture and ginger into mango purée until blended.

Ladle or pour mixture into 8 ¾-cup custard cups, ramekins, or small molds. Loosely cover with plastic wrap and chill 4 hours or up to overnight.

Cut around edges of each panna cotta to loosen. Set each cup in shallow bowl of hot water for 10 seconds. Immediately invert each onto a plate. Spoon the jasmine tea syrup over and around each panna cotta and garnish with flowers or mint sprigs. Makes 8 servings.

JASMINE TEA SYRUP

2 cups water

5 jasmine green tea bags

7 tablespoons sugar

In a medium saucepan bring the water to a boil. Add the tea bags. Let mixture steep 5 minutes and discard tea bags. Add the sugar to tea mixture. Bring the tea mixture to a boil over medium-high heat. Continue boiling until reduced to about 1⅓ cups. Pour mixture into a small heatproof measuring cup or bowl. Cool mixture completely. Cover and chill until ready to use.

Pumpkin Panna Cotta

WITH FRESH POMEGRANATE SAUCE

This dessert is too delicious to reserve for the holidays—instead, serve it up anytime you're feeling festive. The simple pomegranate sauce offsets the smooth pumpkin panna cotta with elegance, both in taste and appearance. You may never make pumpkin pie again.

Place the heavy cream in a medium saucepan. Sprinkle gelatin over the cream. Let stand 5 minutes to soften gelatin. Add the brown sugar. Cook and stir over low heat until both the gelatin and brown sugar are completely dissolved (do not let mixture come to a boil). Whisk in the pumpkin, vanilla, cinnamon, ginger, and cloves until blended.

Ladle or pour mixture into 8 ¾-cup custard cups, ramekins, or small molds. Loosely cover with plastic wrap and chill 4 hours or up to overnight.

Cut around edges of each panna cotta to loosen. Set each cup in shallow bowl of hot water for 10 seconds. Immediately invert each onto a plate. Spoon fresh pomegranate sauce over and around each panna cotta. Makes 8 servings.

2¼ cups heavy whipping cream

2¼ teaspoons unflavored gelatin

½ cup packed light brown sugar

1¼ cups solid pack canned pumpkin purée

1 teaspoon vanilla extract

1½ teaspoons ground cinnamon

1 teaspoon ground ginger

⅛ teaspoon ground cloves

1 recipe Fresh Pomegranate Sauce (see below)

FRESH POMEGRANATE SAUCE

⅔ cup red currant jelly

⅓ cup pomegranate juice (e.g., POM) or cranberry juice cocktail

Seeds from 1 medium pomegranate

Heat jelly and juice in small saucepan just until melted and smooth. Remove from heat, stir in pomegranate seeds. Cool to room temperature.

Fruit Panna Cotta

Banana Panna Cotta

WITH CARAMEL-PECAN DRIZZLE

Humble bananas get sassy in this praline-topped treat. So rich and delicious, this recipe will have everyone skipping dinner and begging for dessert.

Place the peeled banana in a blender or food processor. Purée until very smooth. Measure 1⅔ cups banana purée into 2-cup glass measuring cup; mix in lemon juice and set aside (save any extra banana purée for another use).

Place schnapps or water in small bowl. Sprinkle gelatin over. Let stand 5 minutes to soften gelatin.

Bring the cream and sugar to simmer in heavy, medium saucepan set over medium-high heat, stirring until sugar dissolves. Remove from heat. Add gelatin mixture and whisk until dissolved. Whisk in the banana purée, vanilla, and nutmeg until blended.

Ladle or pour mixture into 8 ¾-cup custard cups, ramekins, or small molds. Loosely cover with plastic wrap and chill 4 hours or up to overnight.

Cut around edges of each panna cotta to loosen. Set each cup in shallow bowl of hot water for 10 seconds. Immediately invert each onto a plate. Spoon the caramel-pecan drizzle around each panna cotta. Makes 8 servings.

4 ripe, large bananas, peeled

2 teaspoons fresh lemon juice

¼ cup banana-flavored schnapps or water

2 teaspoons unflavored gelatin

1¾ cups heavy whipping cream

¼ cup sugar

1 teaspoon vanilla extract

¼ teaspoon ground nutmeg

1 recipe Caramel-Pecan Drizzle (see below)

CARAMEL-PECAN DRIZZLE

1 cup premium caramel sauce

⅔ cup pecans, coarsely chopped and lightly toasted

In a medium saucepan set over moderately-low heat, heat the caramel sauce with the pecans, stirring until warm but not hot.

Sweet Goat Cheese Panna Cotta

WITH ROASTED PLUMS

Intriguingly flavored and not too sweet, this refined dessert is a simple and stylish rendition of the cheese-and-fruit course, all in one.

Place the heavy cream in a medium saucepan. Sprinkle gelatin over the cream. Let stand 5 minutes to soften gelatin.

Add the sugar to saucepan. Cook and stir over low heat until both gelatin and sugar are completely dissolved (do not let mixture come to a boil). Whisk in the goat cheese, sour cream, and vanilla until well-blended and smooth.

Ladle or pour mixture into 8 ¾-cup custard cups, ramekins, or small molds. Loosely cover with plastic wrap and chill 4 hours or up to overnight.

Cut around edges of each panna cotta to loosen. Set each cup in shallow bowl of hot water for 10 seconds. Immediately invert each onto a plate. Spoon the roasted plums and any accumulated juices around each panna cotta. Makes 8 servings.

2 cups heavy whipping cream
2 teaspoons unflavored gelatin
½ cup sugar
8 ounces goat cheese, room temperature
⅔ cup sour cream
1 teaspoon vanilla extract
1 recipe Roasted Plums (see below)

ROASTED PLUMS

2 pounds Italian plums, or other variety, quartered, pits removed
2½ tablespoons packed light brown sugar
⅛ teaspoon freshly ground black pepper

Preheat oven to 425°F. Toss plum halves with brown sugar and pepper; place in an oven-proof skillet. Transfer skillet to oven and roast until plums are soft and juice is bubbling, about 15–20 minutes. Remove from oven. Transfer plums to a medium bowl and cool completely.

Passion Fruit Panna Cotta

Native to tropical regions including Brazil, the West Indies, Africa, and Malaysia, the passion fruit is an egg-shaped berry covered by a thick smooth skin, the size of a small apple and yellow, pink, or purplish-brown in color. It contains a large number of black seeds surrounded by their tegument, which caused the Spanish to nickname it "little pomegranate." The tart-sweet flavor is exquisite and is somewhat reminiscent of guava.

Combine the water and lime juice in small bowl. Sprinkle gelatin over. Let stand 5 minutes to soften gelatin.

Bring cream and sugar to simmer in heavy, medium saucepan over medium-high heat, stirring until sugar dissolves. Remove from heat. Add gelatin mixture, whisking until dissolved. Whisk in the sour cream and 1 cup of the passion fruit purée.

Ladle or pour mixture into 8 ¾-cup custard cups, ramekins, or small molds. Loosely cover with plastic wrap and chill 4 hours or up to overnight.

Cut around edges of each panna cotta to loosen. Set each cup in shallow bowl of hot water for 10 seconds. Immediately invert each onto a plate. Drizzle with some of the remaining passion fruit purée and garnish with lime zest strips and edible tropical flowers. Makes 8 servings.

2 tablespoons water

2 tablespoons fresh lime juice

2⅛ teaspoons unflavored gelatin

1¾ cups heavy whipping cream

½ cup sugar

½ cup sour cream

1 14-ounce package (about 1½ cups) thawed unsweetened passion fruit (maracuyá) purée (e.g., Goya brand), divided use

Garnish: thin strips of lime zest, edible tropical flowers

Mint Julep Panna Cotta

Late Harvest Riesling Panna Cotta

Green Tea Panna Cotta

Crème Fraîche Panna Cotta

Dark Chocolate-Cabernet Panna Cotta

Baba au Rhum Panna Cotta

Limoncello & Mint Panna Cotta

Fuzzy Navel Panna Cotta

Strawberry Daiquiri Panna Cotta

Sherry Panna Cotta

Sangria Panna Cotta

Eggnog Panna Cotta

Ricotta Panna Cotta

Winter Spice Panna Cotta

Margarita Panna Cotta

White Chocolate Amaretto Panna Cotta

Irish Cream Panna Cotta

Cherries Jubilee Panna Cotta

Chapter 4

SPIRITED

PANNA COTTA

Mint Julep Panna Cotta

Inspired by the Kentucky Derby drink of choice, this celebratory dessert is quintessential summertime fare. For a whimsical presentation, consider preparing the panna cotta in barware glasses instead of small molds. Come serving time, simply drizzle the bourbon syrup into each glass and garnish with mint sprigs.

Bring cream, sugar, and mint to simmer in heavy medium saucepan over medium-high heat, stirring until sugar dissolves. Remove from heat. Cover and let steep 20 minutes.

Combine lemon juice and water in small bowl. Sprinkle gelatin over. Let stand 5 minutes to soften gelatin.

Strain mixture through a fine mesh sieve into a large pitcher or measuring cup, pressing on solids. Discard chopped mint. Return cream mixture to saucepan. Rewarm over medium heat for 2 minutes. Add gelatin mixture and whisk until dissolved. Whisk in sour cream.

Ladle or pour mixture into 8 ¾-cup custard cups, ramekins, or small molds. Loosely cover with plastic wrap and chill 4 hours or up to overnight.

Cut around edges of each panna cotta to loosen. Set each cup in shallow bowl of hot water for 10 seconds. Immediately invert each onto a plate. Spoon the bourbon syrup over each panna cotta and garnish with fresh mint sprigs. Makes 8 servings.

2⅔ cups heavy whipping cream

½ cup packed sugar

1 cup packed fresh mint leaves, coarsely chopped

2 tablespoons fresh lemon juice

2 tablespoons water

2 teaspoons unflavored gelatin

¾ cup sour cream

1 recipe Bourbon Syrup (see below)

Garnish: fresh mint sprigs

BOURBON SYRUP

6 tablespoons sugar

6 tablespoons water

½ cup bourbon

Bring sugar and water to a boil in a very small saucepan, stirring until sugar is dissolved, then boil 1 minute. Pour sugar mixture into Pyrex measuring cup or small bowl; stir in bourbon. Cool. Loosely cover and refrigerate until ready to use.

Late Harvest Riesling Panna Cotta

The most highly revered wines made from Riesling are late harvest dessert wines, produced by letting the grapes hang on the vines well past normal picking time. Water is removed from the grapes through evaporation or by freezing, resulting in a wine with profoundly rich layers of flavor and increased sweetness. Panna cotta is an ideal canvas for highlighting Riesling's tropical and floral aromas; the kiwifruit is a bright complement.

1 cup plus 3 tablespoons late harvest Riesling wine, divided use

2 teaspoons unflavored gelatin

2 cups heavy whipping cream

8 tablespoons sugar, divided use

½ cup whole-milk yogurt

6 kiwifruit, peeled, quartered lengthwise, and sliced

Place ¼ cup of the Riesling in small bowl. Sprinkle gelatin over wine. Let stand 5 minutes to soften gelatin.

Bring the cream and 7 tablespoons sugar to simmer in heavy, medium saucepan over medium-high heat, stirring until sugar dissolves. Remove from heat. Add gelatin mixture and whisk until dissolved. Whisk in the yogurt and ¾ cup of the remaining Riesling.

Ladle or pour mixture into 8 wine glasses. Loosely cover with plastic wrap and chill 4 hours or up to overnight.

In a medium bowl combine the kiwifruit, remaining 3 tablespoons Riesling, and remaining tablespoon sugar. Loosely cover and refrigerate until ready to use.

When ready to serve, spoon the kiwi mixture atop each of the panna cotta. Makes 8 servings.

Green Tea Panna Cotta

WITH MIRIN-LIME SYRUP

Matcha, a Japanese form of powdered green tea, is the secret to the vibrant taste and color of both green tea ice cream and this exotic panna cotta. Also known as hiki-cha, it is readily available in Japanese grocery stores and through multiple online cooking sources (see appendix). Be sure to use unsweetened matcha; some varieties of the powder come presweetened. The key ingredient of the accompanying syrup is mirin, a sweet Japanese wine. You can substitute another sweet, floral white wine, such as Riesling or Gewurtstramiener.

Place water in small bowl. Sprinkle gelatin over water. Let stand 5 minutes to soften gelatin.

Bring cream, milk, sugar, and salt just to a simmer in a heavy, medium saucepan over moderate heat, stirring until sugar is dissolved.

Place the matcha in a small bowl. Add 1 cup hot cream mixture in a slow stream, whisking vigorously. Whisk matcha mixture and gelatin mixture into saucepan with remaining cream mixture until gelatin is dissolved.

Ladle or pour mixture into 8 ¾-cup custard cups, ramekins, or small molds. Loosely cover with plastic wrap and chill 4 hours or up to overnight.

Cut around edges of each panna cotta to loosen. Set each cup in shallow bowl of hot water for 10 seconds. Immediately invert each onto a plate. Spoon mirin-lime syrup over and around each panna cotta. Garnish with edible flowers, if desired. Makes 8 servings.

¼ cup water
2 teaspoons unflavored gelatin
2 cups heavy whipping cream
1¼ cups whole milk
½ cup sugar
⅛ teaspoon salt
2 tablespoons matcha (powdered Japanese green tea)
1 recipe Mirin-Lime Syrup (see below)
Garnish: edible flowers

MIRIN-LIME SYRUP

1 cup mirin (sweet Japanese wine)
2 tablespoons fresh lime juice
½ cup sugar
1 2x½-inch strip lime zest

Combine mirin, lime juice, sugar, and lime zest strip in a medium saucepan. Bring to a boil; reduce heat to medium-low and simmer the mixture, stirring occasionally, for 10 minutes, or until it is reduced to about ⅔ cup. Remove the lime zest with slotted spoon. Cool completely. Cover and refrigerate until ready to serve.

Cook's note: This panna cotta is also superb served with the Bittersweet Chocolate Sauce (see page 37) in place of the Mirin-Lime Syrup.

Crème Fraîche Panna Cotta

WITH RED WINE SYRUP

Crème fraîche is thickened cream with a slightly tangy, nutty flavor and velvety rich texture. In other words, it is ideal for the sophisticated simplicity of panna cotta. Crème fraîche is a specialty in France, where the cream is unpasteurized and therefore contains the bacteria necessary to thicken it naturally. In America, where all commercial cream is pasteurized, the fermenting agents necessary for crème fraîche can be obtained by adding buttermilk or sour cream. Crème fraîche is sold in well-stocked grocery stores, as well as specialty and gourmet markets, but is easily made at home, too (see below).

Place the heavy cream in a medium saucepan. Sprinkle gelatin over the cream. Let stand 5 minutes to soften gelatin. Add the sugar. Cook and stir over low heat until both the gelatin and sugar are completely dissolved (do not let mixture come to a boil). Whisk in the crème fraîche, vanilla, and coriander until well-blended.

Ladle or pour mixture into 8 ¾-cup custard cups, ramekins, or small molds. Loosely cover with plastic wrap and chill 4 hours or up to overnight.

Cut around edges of each panna cotta to loosen. Set each cup in shallow bowl of hot water for 10 seconds. Immediately invert each onto a plate. Spoon the red wine syrup around each panna cotta and, if desired, garnish with grapes. Makes 8 servings.

1½ cups heavy cream
2 teaspoons unflavored gelatin
½ cup sugar
2 cups crème fraîche, purchased or homemade (see cook's note below)

1 teaspoon vanilla extract
¼ teaspoon ground coriander
1 recipe Red Wine Syrup (see below)
Garnish: 1½ cups small cluster Champagne table grapes or diced seedless red grapes

RED WINE SYRUP

1 750-ml bottle dry red wine
1 cup sugar

Bring wine and sugar to boil in large saucepan, stirring until sugar dissolves. Boil until reduced to 1 cup, about 17-20 minutes. Cool syrup completely. Cover and chill until cold.

Cook's note: To make homemade crème fraîche, combine 1 cup whipping cream and 2 tablespoons buttermilk in a glass container. Cover and let stand at room temperature (about 70°F) for 8-24 hours, or until very thick. Stir well before covering and refrigerate up to 10 days. Makes about 1 cup crème fraîche. (Recipe may be doubled.)

Dark Chocolate–Cabernet Panna Cotta

WITH CARDAMOM CRÈME ANGLAISE

The ingredients in this intensely flavored panna cotta are anything but shy: decadent bittersweet chocolate, lush cream, Cabernet Sauvignon, and a light sprinkling of spices. The cardamom crème Anglaise provides a smooth, sophisticated counterpoint and is surprisingly simple to prepare.

Place wine in small bowl. Sprinkle gelatin over wine. Let stand 5 minutes to soften gelatin.

In a medium saucepan stir together the sugar and ¾ cup of the cream. Heat over medium heat until hot but not boiling. Add the chopped chocolate to saucepan and whisk until melted and perfectly smooth. Add the wine-gelatin mixture, whisking until gelatin is dissolved. Whisk in the cocoa powder, ginger, cinnamon, and cloves until well-blended and smooth. Whisk in the remaining 1½ cups cream.

Ladle or pour mixture into 8 ¾-cup custard cups, ramekins, or small molds. Loosely cover with plastic wrap and chill 4 hours or up to overnight.

Cut around edges of each panna cotta to loosen. Set each cup in shallow bowl of hot water for 10 seconds. Immediately invert each onto a plate. Spoon the Crème Anglaise around each panna cotta. Makes 8 servings.

1 cup Cabernet Sauvignon
2⅛ teaspoons unflavored gelatin
3 tablespoons sugar
2¼ cups heavy whipping cream, divided use
6 ounces bittersweet chocolate, chopped
2 tablespoons unsweetened cocoa powder (not Dutch process)
¼ teaspoon ground ginger
⅛ teaspoon ground cinnamon
Pinch of ground cloves
1 recipe Cardamom Crème Anglaise (see below)

CARDAMOM CRÈME ANGLAISE

2 cups half and half
½ cup sugar, divided
4 large egg yolks
½ teaspoon ground cardamom
1 teaspoon vanilla extract

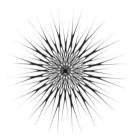

Place the half and half and ¼ cup sugar in heavy, medium saucepan over medium-high heat. Bring mixture to simmer.

Whisk egg yolks and remaining ¼ cup sugar in medium bowl. Gradually whisk in hot cream mixture and cardamom. Return mixture to same saucepan. Stir over medium-low heat until custard thickens and leaves path on back of spoon when finger is drawn across, stirring constantly, about 2 minutes (do not boil). Remove from heat and whisk in vanilla. Cover and chill until cold, about 3 hours. Strain into medium pitcher. Makes 2 cups.

Cook's note: The Cardamom Crème Anglaise can be made 2 days ahead. Cover and refrigerate.

Baba au Rhum Panna Cotta

A classic French dessert, baba au rhum is a rich currant-studded yeast cake soaked in a rum syrup. Here it serves as sweet inspiration for panna cotta, with custard taking the place of cake. Traditional baba molds—small, tall, and cylindrical—make excellent panna cotta molds, whether for this recipe or any other panna cotta recipe in this collection.

Place water in small bowl. Sprinkle gelatin over water. Let stand 5 minutes to soften gelatin.

In a medium saucepan stir together the sugar and cream. Heat over medium heat until hot but not boiling. Add gelatin mixture and stir until gelatin is dissolved. Remove from heat. Stir in sour cream, vanilla, and nutmeg.

Ladle or pour mixture into 8 ¾-cup custard cups, ramekins, or small molds (such as individual baba molds). Loosely cover with plastic wrap and chill 4 hours or up to overnight.

To serve, immerse bottom half of ramekin or custard cup in hot water about 15 seconds. Run a clean small knife around edge to loosen. Invert onto dessert plate. Repeat with remaining desserts. Spoon rum-currant sauce over each panna cotta and serve. Makes 8 servings.

¼ cup water

2⅛ teaspoons unflavored gelatin

½ cup sugar

2¼ cups well-chilled heavy whipping cream

1 cup sour cream

1½ teaspoons vanilla extract

¼ teaspoon ground nutmeg

1 recipe Rum-Currant Sauce (see below)

RUM-CURRANT SAUCE

½ cup sugar

1 cup water

⅓ cup dark rum

½ teaspoon vanilla extract

½ cup currants

In a small saucepan combine the sugar and the water. Bring the mixture to a boil, stirring until the sugar is dissolved, and simmer the syrup for about 3 minutes or until sugar is completely dissolved. Remove the pan from the heat and stir in the rum, vanilla, and currants. Loosely cover and cool to room temperature.

Limoncello & Mint Panna Cotta

Sipping ice cold limoncello—the bittersweet Italian liqueur made from fermented Sorrento lemons—is pleasure enough, but savoring it as part of a fresh, mint-infused panna cotta is citrus heaven. Refreshing and light, it is an incomparable dessert for lemon lovers.

Place heavy cream, sugar, and mint leaves in medium saucepan. Bring to a simmer over medium-high heat, stirring until sugar is dissolved; remove from heat. Cover and let steep 20 minutes. Remove mint leaves with a slotted spoon; discard leaves. Add lemon zest to cream.

Place the lemon juice in small bowl; sprinkle gelatin over (do not stir). Let stand 5 minutes to soften gelatin.

Reheat cream mixture over medium-high heat. Remove from heat and whisk in gelatin mixture until blended and gelatin is dissolved.

Ladle or pour mixture into 8 short bar glasses or other decorative glasses. Loosely cover with plastic wrap and chill 4 hours or up to overnight.

Just before serving, place one lemon slice atop each panna cotta, drizzle with 1 tablespoon chilled limoncello, and garnish with a mint sprig. Makes 8 servings.

3¼ cups heavy whipping cream

½ cup sugar

1 cup loosely packed fresh mint leaves

1 teaspoon finely grated lemon zest

¼ cup fresh lemon juice

2 teaspoons unflavored gelatin

8 thin slices lemon

½ cup chilled limoncello

8 small fresh mint sprigs

Fuzzy Navel Panna Cotta

If you have ever wondered how the fuzzy navel cocktail got its name, consider the mystery solved: it's merely a conflation of peach "fuzz" and "navel" orange. The combination of flavors couldn't be better matched, as this delightful panna cotta illustrates.

Place ¼ cup of the peach liqueur in small bowl. Sprinkle gelatin over liqueur. Let stand 5 minutes to soften gelatin.

Bring the cream, sugar, and orange zest to simmer in heavy, medium saucepan over medium-high heat, stirring until sugar dissolves. Remove from heat and add the gelatin mixture; whisk until dissolved. Whisk in the orange juice until blended.

Ladle or pour mixture into 8 ¾-cup custard cups, ramekins, or small molds. Loosely cover with plastic wrap and chill 4 hours or up to overnight.

Cut around edges of each panna cotta to loosen. Set each cup in shallow bowl of hot water for 10 seconds. Immediately invert each onto a plate. Serve by spooning some of the remaining ¼ cup peach liqueur over each panna cotta and sprinkling the plates with diced peaches. Makes 8 servings.

½ cup peach liqueur or peach schnapps, divided use

2 teaspoons unflavored gelatin

2¼ cups heavy whipping cream

¼ cup sugar

1 teaspoon finely grated orange zest

1¼ cups freshly squeezed orange juice, strained

Garnish: 1½ cups diced fresh peaches

Strawberry Daiquiri Panna Cotta

This gorgeous dessert is sweet with fresh strawberries and enlivened with a splash of tequila. With its juicy fruit, creamy custard, and pale pink hue, it will please any dessert lover.

4½ cups halved, hulled strawberries, divided use

¼ cup light rum

2 teaspoons unflavored gelatin

1½ cups heavy whipping cream

½ cup sugar

1 teaspoon finely grated lime zest

⅔ cup sour cream

3 tablespoons fresh lime juice

3 tablespoons honey

Garnish: coarse sugar, lime wedges, freshly grated lime zest

Place 2 cups of the strawberries in a food processor and process until smooth. Pour purée through a fine mesh strainer, pressing with rubber spatula to extract as much purée as possible. Reserve the strained purée and discard the seeds in strainer.

Place rum in small bowl. Sprinkle gelatin over rum. Let stand 5 minutes to soften gelatin.

Bring the cream, sugar, and lime zest to simmer in heavy, medium saucepan over medium-high heat, stirring until sugar dissolves. Remove from heat and add the gelatin mixture; whisk until dissolved. Whisk in the puréed strawberries, sour cream, and lime juice until blended.

Ladle or pour mixture into 8 margarita glasses. Loosely cover with plastic wrap and chill 4 hours or up to overnight.

Gently toss remaining 2½ cups strawberry halves and honey in medium bowl to blend. Let stand at room temperature 30 minutes. Chill until ready to use.

Spread the coarse sugar on a small plate. Rub a lime wedge around the edge of each glass; dip glass in coarse sugar to coat rim. Spoon the strawberries and their accumulated juices on top of each panna cotta. Garnish with lime zest. Makes 8 servings.

Sherry Panna Cotta

WITH GOLDEN WALNUT SAUCE

Although sherry originates from the Andalusian region of Spain, the sweet variety of this fortified wine, often labeled cream or golden sherry, is recognized as a distinctively British aperitif. Here it acts as a stealth ingredient, enhancing the marriage of sweet cream and toasted walnuts.

Place sherry in small bowl. Sprinkle gelatin over sherry. Let stand 5 minutes to soften gelatin.

Place heavy cream and brown sugar in medium saucepan. Bring to a simmer over medium-high heat, stirring until sugar is dissolved; remove from heat. Whisk in gelatin mixture until blended and gelatin is dissolved. Whisk in sour cream, vanilla, and nutmeg until blended.

Ladle or pour mixture into 8 ¾-cup custard cups, ramekins, or small molds. Loosely cover with plastic wrap and chill 4 hours or up to overnight.

Cut around edges of each panna cotta to loosen. Set each cup in shallow bowl of hot water for 10 seconds. Immediately invert each onto a plate. Serve with golden walnut sauce. Makes 8 servings.

¼ cup sweet or cream sherry
2 teaspoons unflavored gelatin
2¾ cups heavy whipping cream
½ cup packed light brown sugar
½ cup sour cream
1 teaspoon pure vanilla extract
¼ teaspoon freshly grated nutmeg
1 recipe Golden Walnut Sauce (see below)

GOLDEN WALNUT SAUCE

⅔ cup golden syrup (e.g., Lyle's brand) or mild-flavored honey
¼ cup sweet sherry
3 tablespoons chopped golden raisins
1 tablespoon fresh lemon juice
1 teaspoon vanilla
¾ cup chopped toasted walnuts

In a small saucepan simmer golden syrup, sherry, raisins, and lemon juice, covered, stirring occasionally, until sauce thickens slightly (about 3–4 minutes). Stir vanilla and walnuts into sauce. Let cool to lukewarm or room temperature.

Sangria Panna Cotta

The inspiration for this voluptuous panna cotta is Sangria, the deep red beverage made from red wine, fruit, and brandy. You can make the panna cotta in molds and spoon the sauce and fruit around the un-molded panna cotta, but it is simply gorgeous when prepared and served in oversized martini glasses or goblets, as described below.

Combine brandy and lemon juice in small bowl. Sprinkle gelatin over. Let stand 5 minutes to soften gelatin.

Place heavy cream, sugar, lemon zest, and orange zest in medium saucepan. Bring to a simmer over medium-high heat, stirring until sugar is dissolved; remove from heat. Whisk in gelatin mixture until blended and gelatin is dissolved. Whisk in sour cream until blended.

Ladle or pour mixture into 8 goblets or other stemmed glasses. Loosely cover with plastic wrap and chill 4 hours or up to overnight. Just before serving, divide sangria sauce atop each of the glasses of panna cotta. Makes 8 servings.

2 tablespoons brandy
2 tablespoons fresh lemon juice
2 teaspoons unflavored gelatin
2¼ cups heavy whipping cream
½ cup sugar
½ teaspoon finely grated lemon zest
½ teaspoon finely grated orange zest
1 cup sour cream
1 recipe Sangria Sauce (see next column)

SANGRIA SAUCE

1 cup fruity red wine (e.g., Zinfandel)
¼ cup fresh orange juice
3 tablespoons brandy
1 tablespoon fresh lemon juice
¼ cup sugar
2 firm-ripe peaches, cut into thin wedges
1 pint strawberries, hulled, and diced

Stir together wine, orange juice, brandy, lemon juice, and sugar (to taste) in a bowl. Stir in strawberries and peaches and let macerate at room temperature 1 hour, then chill until cold, up to 1 hour but no longer. (Fruit will become too soft if it steeps for more than 2 hours.)

Eggnog Panna Cotta

WITH BUTTERED RUM SAUCE

The understated, familiar flavor of eggnog in custard form is at once both delicate and rich, thanks in part to a decadent buttered rum sauce topping. One bite will recapture all of your favorite winter holiday memories.

Place rum in small bowl. Sprinkle gelatin over rum. Let stand 5 minutes to soften gelatin.

Bring cream and sugar to simmer in heavy, medium saucepan over medium-high heat, stirring until sugar dissolves. Remove from heat. Add gelatin mixture and whisk until gelatin is dissolved. Whisk in eggnog, sour cream, vanilla, nutmeg, and cinnamon.

Ladle or pour mixture into 8 ¾-cup custard cups, ramekins, or small molds. Loosely cover with plastic wrap and chill 4 hours or up to overnight.

Cut around edges of each panna cotta to loosen. Set each cup in shallow bowl of hot water for 10 seconds. Immediately invert each onto a plate. Heat buttered rum sauce in a small saucepan set over low heat, or in microwave, until warm but not hot. Spoon buttered rum sauce around each panna cotta and, if desired, freshly grate a small amount of nutmeg around outer edge of each plate. Makes 8 servings.

¼ cup dark rum
2 teaspoons unflavored gelatin
¾ cup heavy whipping cream
3½ tablespoons sugar

2 cups eggnog (not reduced-fat variety)
½ cup sour cream
1 teaspoon vanilla extract
½ teaspoon freshly grated nutmeg
¼ teaspoon ground cinnamon
1 recipe Buttered Rum Sauce (see below)
Optional garnish: freshly grated nutmeg

BUTTERED RUM SAUCE

1 cup firmly packed dark brown sugar
½ cup (1 stick) unsalted butter
½ cup heavy whipping cream
2½ tablespoons dark rum

In a heavy, small saucepan set over medium heat, stir the brown sugar and butter until melted and smooth, about 2 minutes. Add the cream and rum and bring to simmer. Simmer until sauce thickens and is reduced to 1½ cups, about 5 minutes. Cool to warm. Serve warm with panna cotta. (Can be prepared up to 2 days ahead. Cover and refrigerate. Rewarm before serving.)

Ricotta Panna Cotta

WITH SAMBUCA-POACHED FRESH FIGS

The slightly grainy texture of fresh ricotta cheese makes a sublime foil to sambuca-poached figs. Sambuca is an anise-flavored liqueur, produced by the infusion of witch elder bush and licorice, sweetened with sugar and enhanced with a secret combination of herbs and spices. Be sure to select white sambuca, which is the traditional and generally more popular variety. It has a mellower licorice taste and lighter body than that of black sambuca.

Place the half and half in a medium saucepan. Sprinkle gelatin over. Let stand 5 minutes to soften gelatin. Add the sugar to the saucepan. Cook and stir over low heat until both the gelatin and sugar are completely dissolved (do not let mixture come to a boil).

Place ricotta cheese, vanilla, and half of the cream mixture in blender or food processor container; cover. Blend until puréed. Stir in remaining cream.

Ladle or pour mixture into 8 ¾-cup custard cups, ramekins, or small molds. Loosely cover with plastic wrap and chill 4 hours or up to overnight.

Cut around edges of each panna cotta to loosen. Set each cup in shallow bowl of hot water for 10 seconds. Immediately invert each onto a plate. Spoon the Sambuca-poached figs and their liquid around each panna cotta and sprinkle with a few pine nuts. Makes 8 servings.

2 cups half and half
2 teaspoons unflavored gelatin
½ cup sugar
1½ cups whole-milk ricotta cheese
1 teaspoon vanilla extract
1 recipe Sambuca-Poached Fresh Figs (see below)
⅓ cup pine nuts, lightly toasted, cooled

SAMBUCA-POACHED FRESH FIGS

¾ cup Sambuca (white variety)
2 tablespoons honey
12 firm-ripe fresh purple figs, stemmed and quartered

Simmer Sambuca with honey in a saucepan (pan should be just large enough to hold figs upright), stirring until sugar is dissolved. Poach figs at a bare simmer, covered, 5 minutes. Figs will not be covered by liquid.) Cool in liquid.

Winter Spice Panna Cotta

WITH CABERNET-CARAMEL SAUCE

The perfect no-fuss dessert for cold-weather entertaining, this panna cotta is redolent with the spices of the season. The cabernet caramel sauce is a quintessentially rich and cozy accompaniment.

Bring the cream, brown sugar, cinnamon sticks, cloves, and allspice berries to simmer in heavy, medium saucepan over medium-high heat, stirring until sugar dissolves. Remove from heat. Cover and let steep 30 minutes.

Place water in small bowl. Sprinkle gelatin over water. Let stand 5 minutes to soften gelatin.

Strain cream mixture through a fine mesh sieve into a large pitcher or measuring cup, pressing on solids. Discard cinnamon sticks, cloves, and allspice. Return cream mixture to saucepan; rewarm over medium heat for 2–3 minutes until very warm but not hot. Add gelatin mixture and whisk until gelatin is dissolved. Whisk in buttermilk.

Ladle or pour mixture into 8 ¾-cup custard cups, ramekins, or small molds. Loosely cover with plastic wrap and chill 4 hours or up to overnight.

Cut around edges of each panna cotta to loosen. Set each cup in shallow bowl of hot water for 10 seconds. Immediately invert onto plate. Spoon cabernet caramel sauce around each panna cotta. Makes 8 servings.

2 cups whipping cream
½ cup packed light brown sugar
6 whole cinnamon sticks
8 whole cloves, slightly crushed
2 allspice berries, slightly crushed
¼ cup water
2 teaspoons unflavored gelatin
1¼ cups low-fat buttermilk
1 recipe Cabernet Caramel Sauce (see below)

CABERNET-CARAMEL SAUCE

¼ cup (½ stick) unsalted butter
1 cup sugar
½ cup heavy whipping cream
¾ cup Cabernet Sauvignon
1 teaspoon vanilla extract

Place the butter and sugar in a small saucepan set over medium-high heat. Cook and stir continuously about 7–8 minutes until sugar is melted and caramelized. Remove pan from heat; stir in cream (it will splutter a bit), blending. Return to medium heat and slowly whisk in wine. Remove from heat and whisk in vanilla. Cool to lukewarm or refrigerate, covered, until ready to use. Rewarm sauce slightly over low heat before serving.

Margarita Panna Cotta

WITH MANGO "SALSA"

Spark up your next fiesta. This festive, yet elegant, dessert takes its cues from a range of authentic South-of-the-Border flavors: tequila, fresh lime, mango, mint, and a hit of heat. You can prepare these pretty panna cotte in traditional molds, but they are extra special when prepared, as I suggest, in margarita glasses that are dipped in lime juice and coarse sugar just before serving.

Combine tequila, Grand Marnier, and 3 tablespoons of the lime juice in small bowl. Sprinkle gelatin over. Let stand 5 minutes to soften gelatin.

Bring cream, ½ cup regular sugar, lime zest, and salt to simmer in heavy, medium saucepan over medium-high heat, stirring until sugar dissolves. Remove from heat. Whisk in gelatin mixture until gelatin is dissolved. Whisk in sour cream and cinnamon.

Ladle or pour mixture into 8 margarita glasses. Loosely cover with plastic wrap and chill 4 hours or up to overnight.

Place the coarse sugar in a shallow dish or saucer. Place the remaining 3 tablespoons lime juice in a second shallow dish or saucer. Dip the rims of each glass in lime juice, then in coarse sugar. Top each panna cotta with mango "salsa." Makes 8 servings.

3 tablespoons tequila (preferably gold)
3 tablespoons Grand Marnier or other orange liqueur
6 tablespoons fresh lime juice, divided use
2 teaspoons unflavored gelatin

2 cups heavy whipping cream
½ cup sugar
¾ teaspoon finely grated lime zest
⅛ teaspoon salt
1 cup sour cream
¼ teaspoon ground cinnamon
⅔ cup coarse sugar
1 recipe Mango "Salsa" (see below)

MANGO "SALSA"

2 cups fresh mango cut into ½-inch cubes
3 tablespoons thinly slivered fresh mint
½ of 1 jalapeño pepper, seeded and minced
2 tablespoons fresh lime juice
1 tablespoon light brown sugar

Place the mango, mint, jalapeño, lime juice, and brown sugar in a non-reactive mixing bowl, but do not mix them until 5 minutes before you are ready to serve. Makes about 2 cups.

White Chocolate Amaretto Panna Cotta

Delicate almond flavor and fine white chocolate lend this panna cotta cosmopolitan flair.

Place ¼ cup of the amaretto in small bowl. Sprinkle gelatin over amaretto. Let stand 5 minutes to soften gelatin.

Bring the sugar and ¾ cup of the cream to simmer in heavy, medium saucepan over medium-high heat, stirring until sugar dissolves. Remove from heat and add the chopped white chocolate, stirring until melted and perfectly smooth. Add gelatin mixture, whisking until dissolved. Whisk in sour cream and remaining cream.

Ladle or pour mixture into 8 ¾-cup custard cups, ramekins, or small molds. Loosely cover with plastic wrap and chill 4 hours or up to overnight.

Cut around edges of each panna cotta to loosen. Set each cup in shallow bowl of hot water for 10 seconds. Immediately invert each onto a plate. Serve by spooning some of the remaining ¼ cup amaretto over each panna cotta and sprinkling the plates with toasted almonds. Makes 8 servings.

½ cup Amaretto, divided use

2⅛ teaspoons unflavored gelatin

2 tablespoons sugar

2½ cups heavy whipping cream, divided use

6 ounces good-quality white chocolate, chopped

⅔ cup sour cream

Garnish: ½ cup sliced almonds, lightly toasted and cooled

Irish Cream Panna Cotta

WITH IRISH CHOCOLATE SAUCE

The honeyed chocolate-toffee flavor of Irish Cream liqueur could not find a better dessert vehicle than panna cotta. An easily assembled milk chocolate sauce, spiked with more of the liqueur sends this confection straight over the top. For a whimsical presentation, chill the panna cotta mixture in Irish coffee glasses and serve by spooning the Irish Chocolate Sauce on top.

Place liqueur in small bowl. Sprinkle gelatin over liqueur. Let stand 5 minutes to soften gelatin.

Place cream and brown sugar in medium saucepan. Bring to a simmer over medium-high heat, stirring until sugar is dissolved; remove from heat. Whisk in gelatin mixture until blended and gelatin is dissolved. Whisk in sour cream and vanilla extract until blended.

Ladle or pour mixture into 8 ¾-cup custard cups, ramekins, or small molds. Loosely cover with plastic wrap and chill 4 hours or up to overnight.

Cut around edges of each panna cotta to loosen. Set each cup in shallow bowl of hot water for 10 seconds. Immediately invert each onto a plate. Serve with Irish chocolate sauce. Makes 8 servings.

6 tablespoons Irish Cream liqueur
2 teaspoons unflavored gelatin
2½ cups heavy whipping cream
⅓ cup packed light brown sugar
¾ cup sour cream
1 teaspoon vanilla extract
1 recipe Irish Chocolate Sauce (see below)

IRISH CHOCOLATE SAUCE

6 ounces good-quality milk chocolate, finely chopped
¾ cup heavy whipping cream
3 tablespoons light corn syrup
3 tablespoons Irish cream liqueur

Place the chocolate in a small metal bowl. Combine the cream and corn syrup in a heavy, small non-reactive saucepan and bring to a simmer. Pour the liquid over the chocolate and allow it to sit for 3–4 minutes or until the chocolate has melted. Add the liqueur and whisk to combine. Allow the sauce to cool slightly, then pour into a bowl or other container. (Stored in the refrigerator, tightly covered, the sauce will keep for up to 2 weeks. Rewarm sauce slightly in top of a double boiler or in the microwave.)

Cherries Jubilee Panna Cotta

A fuss-free, sweet-tart cherry sauce surrounds a Cognac-accented panna cotta, creating a scrumptious dessert that lives up to its jubilant name.

Combine Cognac and water in small bowl. Sprinkle gelatin over. Let stand 5 minutes to soften gelatin.

Place heavy cream and sugar in medium saucepan. Bring to a simmer over medium-high heat, stirring until sugar is dissolved; remove from heat. Whisk in gelatin mixture until blended and gelatin is dissolved. Whisk in sour cream, vanilla, and almond extract until blended.

Ladle or pour mixture into 8 ¾-cup custard cups, ramekins, or small molds. Loosely cover with plastic wrap and chill 4 hours or up to overnight.

Cut around edges of each panna cotta to loosen. Set each cup in shallow bowl of hot water for 10 seconds. Immediately invert each onto a plate. Serve with the cherry-Cognac topping and sprinkle with toasted almonds. Makes 8 servings.

2 tablespoons Cognac or other brandy

2 tablespoons water

2 teaspoons unflavored gelatin

2¾ cups heavy whipping cream

½ cup sugar

½ cup sour cream

1 teaspoon vanilla extract

¼ teaspoon almond extract

1 recipe Cherry-Cognac Topping (see below)

½ cup sliced almonds, lightly toasted

CHERRY-COGNAC TOPPING

1 cup cherry preserves

¼ teaspoon cinnamon

6 tablespoons Cognac or other brandy

Melt preserves in heavy small saucepan over low heat, stirring frequently. Mix in cinnamon and Cognac. Cool to room temperature.

Chapter 5

ENLIGHTENED

PANNA COTTA

Chocolate Truffle Panna Cotta

This panna cotta is the little black dress of light desserts: chic, sophisticated, and the perfect fit for any occasion. A double dose of cocoa powder—both in the custard and the sauce—is the secret to keeping this dessert light in fat and calories but heavy with deep dark chocolate flavor.

Place water in small bowl. Sprinkle gelatin over water. Let stand 5 minutes to soften gelatin.

Place evaporated milk, cocoa powder, and brown sugar in heavy, medium saucepan. Bring to a simmer over medium-high heat, stirring until sugar is dissolved; remove from heat. Whisk in gelatin mixture until blended and gelatin is dissolved. Whisk in sour cream and vanilla extract until blended.

Ladle or pour mixture into 8 ¾-cup custard cups, ramekins, or small molds. Loosely cover with plastic wrap and chill 4 hours or up to overnight.

Cut around edges of each panna cotta to loosen. Set each cup in shallow bowl of hot water for 10 seconds. Immediately invert each onto a plate. Drizzle with Dark Chocolate Sauce. Makes 8 servings.

¼ cup water
2 teaspoons unflavored gelatin
2¼ cups evaporated fat-free milk (from 2 12-ounce cans)
⅔ cup unsweetened cocoa powder (not Dutch process)
½ cup packed dark brown sugar
1 cup reduced-fat (not fat-free) sour cream
1 teaspoon vanilla extract
1 recipe Dark Chocolate Sauce (see below)

DARK CHOCOLATE SAUCE

2 tablespoons unsalted butter
⅔ cup water
1½ tablespoons instant espresso powder
⅔ cup packed dark brown sugar
1 cup unsweetened cocoa powder (not Dutch process)
Pinch of salt
1 teaspoon vanilla

Cut butter into pieces. In a heavy, medium saucepan heat water, espresso powder, and brown sugar over moderate heat, whisking until sugar is dissolved. Add cocoa powder and salt, whisking until smooth. Add butter and vanilla, whisking until butter is melted. Cool to room temperature. (Note: Sauce will keep, covered and chilled, for 1 week. Rewarm sauce in microwave for 30 seconds on high before serving.)

Vanilla Cream Panna Cotta

WITH TART CHERRY SAUCE

In the world of desserts, this uncomplicated panna cotta strikes harmonious balance: not too rich or too sweet. Fragrant with vanilla, the silken custard is tempered by the tart-sweetness of the cherry sauce.

Place water in small bowl. Sprinkle gelatin over water. Let stand 5 minutes to soften gelatin.

Place evaporated milk and powdered sugar in medium saucepan. Bring to a simmer over medium-high heat, stirring until blended and milk is very warm; remove from heat. Whisk in gelatin mixture until blended and gelatin is dissolved. Whisk in sour cream and vanilla until blended.

Ladle or pour mixture into 8 ¾-cup custard cups, ramekins, or small molds. Loosely cover with plastic wrap and chill 4 hours or up to overnight.

Cut around edges of each panna cotta to loosen. Set each cup in shallow bowl of hot water for 10 seconds. Immediately invert each onto a plate. Serve with tart cherry sauce. Makes 8 servings.

¼ cup water

2 teaspoons unflavored gelatin

1¾ cups evaporated fat-free milk (from 2 12-ounce cans)

½ cup powdered sugar

1½ cups reduced-fat (not fat-free) sour cream

1½ teaspoons vanilla extract

1 recipe Tart Cherry Sauce (see below)

TART CHERRY SAUCE

2 15-ounce cans red tart pie cherries (e.g., Oregon® brand canned fruit), drained, ½ cup syrup reserved

1 teaspoon cornstarch mixed with 1 tablespoon water

Drop of almond extract

In a saucepan bring cherries and reserved syrup to a boil. Stir in the cornstarch mixture until blended. Simmer sauce 2 minutes. Remove from heat and stir in almond extract. Cool to room temperature.

Enlightened Panna Cotta

Ricotta-Honey Panna Cotta

WITH FRESH BERRIES

An assortment of sumptuous, summer berries frame this elegant panna cotta. The honey in the custard adds a luxurious floral sweetness, the ricotta, a velvet-smooth texture.

Blend the ricotta, ¾ cup milk, ½ cup honey, and almond extract in a blender set on medium speed until smooth. Transfer mixture to a medium bowl. Set aside momentarily.

Place the lemon zest and remaining ¾ cup milk in small saucepan. Sprinkle gelatin over. Let stand 5 minutes to soften gelatin. Bring to a simmer over medium heat, stirring until gelatin is dissolved. Whisk the hot milk mixture into the ricotta mixture until blended.

Ladle or pour mixture into 8 ¾-cup custard cups, ramekins, or small molds. Loosely cover with plastic wrap and chill 4 hours or up to overnight.

Cut around edges of each panna cotta to loosen. Set each cup in shallow bowl of hot water for 10 seconds. Immediately invert each onto a plate. Serve panna cotta with fresh berries, drizzled with remaining 3 tablespoons honey. Makes 8 servings.

2 cups fat-free ricotta cheese
1½ cups low-fat milk, divided use
½ cup plus 3 tablespoons honey, divided use
¼ teaspoon pure almond extract
1 teaspoon grated lemon zest
2 teaspoons unflavored gelatin
3 cups assorted fresh berries of your choice

Thai Coconut Panna Cotta

Think light desserts are bland? Then this panna cotta is a must-make. A refined mingling of Thai-inspired flavors—ginger, lime, fresh mint, and fresh basil—are tied together by the cool tropical notes of light coconut milk. The result? A finale with "wow."

Place 4 tablespoons of the lime juice in small bowl. Sprinkle gelatin over juice. Let stand 5 minutes to soften gelatin.

Bring lite coconut milk, ½ cup sugar, and lime zest to simmer in medium saucepan, stirring until sugar dissolves. Add gelatin mixture and whisk until gelatin is dissolved. Whisk in the sour cream, coconut extract, and ginger until smooth.

Ladle or pour mixture into 8 ¾-cup custard cups, ramekins, or small molds. Loosely cover with plastic wrap and chill 4 hours or up to overnight.

In a medium bowl toss the mangoes, mint, basil, remaining tablespoon lime juice, and remaining tablespoon sugar. Chill until ready to use.

Cut around edges of each panna cotta to loosen. Set each cup in shallow bowl of hot water for 10 seconds. Immediately invert each onto a plate. Serve with the chilled mango mixture. Makes 8 servings.

5 tablespoons fresh lime juice, divided use

2⅛ teaspoons unflavored gelatin

2 cups canned lite coconut milk (from 2 14-ounce cans)

½ cup plus 1 tablespoon sugar, divided use

1 teaspoon finely grated lime zest

1¼ cups reduced-fat (not fat-free) sour cream

1 teaspoon coconut extract

1 teaspoon ground ginger

2 medium-large ripe mangoes, peeled, cut into small cubes

2 tablespoons sliced fresh mint leaves

1 tablespoon sliced fresh basil leaves

Mandarin Orange Panna Cotta

The bright and sunny flavor of this mandarin orange panna cotta will steal the spotlight at any supper party. No one will ever guess it is a light confection.

Place ½ cup of the orange juice into a heavy, medium saucepan. Sprinkle 1 teaspoon of the gelatin over juice. Let stand 5 minutes to soften gelatin.

Bring juice to a simmer over medium-high heat, whisking until gelatin is dissolved. Whisk in remaining juice and cool 10 minutes. Ladle or pour mixture into 6 martini or wine glasses. Loosely cover with plastic wrap and chill at least 1 hour to set.

Place milk and orange zest in a heavy, medium saucepan. Sprinkle the remaining 1¾ teaspoons gelatin over the milk. Let stand 5 minutes to soften gelatin. Add the sugar and bay leaves to saucepan. Bring to a simmer over medium-high heat, stirring until sugar and gelatin are dissolved. Cover and let steep 30 minutes. Remove and discard bay leaves. Whisk in chilled buttermilk until blended.

Carefully ladle or pour buttermilk mixture into the glasses with the orange gelatin. Loosely cover with plastic wrap and chill 4 hours or up to overnight.

Serve the parfaits with the chilled mandarin orange segments on top. Makes 6 servings.

1½ cups freshly squeezed, strained orange juice, divided use

2¾ teaspoons unflavored gelatin, divided use

1 cup lowfat milk

1 teaspoon finely grated orange zest

⅓ cup sugar

2 California bay leaves (or 4 Mediterranean bay leaves)

2 cups lowfat buttermilk, well chilled

1 11-ounce can mandarin orange segments, drained and chilled

Root Beer Float Panna Cotta

Creamy vanilla custard layered with root beer gelee is the kind of sweet that brings to mind an old-style soda fountain counter, where tempting confections were the order of the day. A nostalgic treat, this fanciful version of the root beer float is impossible to resist.

Place 8 tall parfait glasses on a baking sheet. Set aside.

Make the gelee: Pour ½ bottle of root beer into a medium-size bowl. Sprinkle gelatin over. Let stand 5 minutes to soften gelatin.

Warm the remaining ½ bottle of diet root beer in small saucepan until hot, but not boiling. Add the gelatin root beer to the hot root beer and whisk together. Add remaining full bottle of root beer, gently stirring to combine. Ladle or pour mixture into the bottom of 8 tall parfait glasses (about ¼ cup per glass). Chill until set.

Make the vanilla panna cotta: Place water in small bowl. Sprinkle gelatin over water. Let stand 5 minutes to soften gelatin.

Bring evaporated milk and powered sugar to simmer in heavy, medium saucepan over medium-high heat, until very warm. Remove from heat. Add gelatin mixture and whisk until gelatin is dissolved. Whisk in sour cream and vanilla. Ladle or pour panna cotta mixture evenly among glasses atop root beer gelee (about ¼ cup per glass). Cover and chill at least 4 hours or up to overnight.

Make the granita: Pour the 12-ounce bottle of root beer into a shallow freezer-proof dish, approximately 4 by 8 inches. Place dish in freezer and scrape with a fork every 30 minutes, until frozen.

To serve, scoop the granita and place on top of each panna cotta. Makes 8 servings.

ROOT BEER GELEE

| 2 12-ounce bottles root beer |
| 1 tablespoon unflavored gelatin |

VANILLA PANNA COTTA

| ¼ cup water |
| 2¼ teaspoons unflavored gelatin |
| 2 cups canned evaporated fat-free milk (from 2 12-ounce cans) |
| ½ cup powered sugar |
| 1½ cups reduced-fat (not fat-free) sour cream |
| 1½ teaspoons vanilla extract |

ROOT BEER GRANITA

| 1 12-ounce bottle root beer |

Enlightened Panna Cotta

Ginger & Brown Sugar Panna Cotta

WITH CARAMELIZED PINEAPPLE

Not just for baking, brown sugar is the dark star in this spiced panna cotta, adding sweet depth to the custard. The caramelized pineapple is a perfect foil and surprisingly simple to prepare when you start with a pretrimmed, precored pineapple from the supermarket produce section.

Place water in small bowl. Sprinkle gelatin over water. Let stand 5 minutes to soften gelatin.

Place evaporated milk and brown sugar in medium saucepan. Bring to a simmer over medium-high heat, stirring until sugar is dissolved; remove from heat. Whisk in gelatin mixture until blended and gelatin is dissolved. Whisk in sour cream, ginger, and vanilla until blended.

Ladle or pour mixture into 8 ¾-cup custard cups, ramekins, or small molds. Loosely cover with plastic wrap and chill 4 hours or up to overnight.

Cut around edges of each panna cotta to loosen. Set each cup in shallow bowl of hot water for 10 seconds. Immediately invert each onto a plate. Spoon pineapple and accumulated juices around each panna cotta. Makes 8 servings.

¼ cup water
2 teaspoons unflavored gelatin
1 12-ounce can evaporated fat-free milk
½ cup packed dark brown sugar
2 cups reduced-fat (not fat-free) sour cream
2 teaspoons ground ginger
1 teaspoon vanilla extract
1 recipe Caramelized Pineapple (see below)

CARAMELIZED PINEAPPLE

1 fresh, peeled, and precored pineapple, cut into chunks
½ cup packed dark brown sugar

Preheat broiler. Line a large baking sheet with foil. Arrange pineapple chunks close together in single layer on prepared baking sheet. Pat pineapple wedges with paper towels to remove excess moisture. Sprinkle brown sugar over pineapple.

Broil pineapple until brown sugar caramelizes, watching closely to avoid burning and rotating baking sheet to broil evenly, about 3 minutes. Transfer pineapple and any accumulated juices to a bowl and cool to room temperature.

Chocolate Amaretti Panna Cotta

WITH FRESH FRUIT

Amaretti are petite Italian cookies that get their traditional crunch from ground almonds and egg whites, making them close cousins to French meringues. They are often used as a base for a variety of custard desserts, from trifle to tiramisu; this chocolate-almond panna cotta follows suit, but with a much lighter fat and calorie profile.

Place rum in small bowl. Sprinkle gelatin over rum. Let stand 5 minutes to soften gelatin.

Place evaporated milk and brown sugar in medium saucepan. Bring to a simmer over medium-high heat, stirring until sugar is dissolved; remove from heat. Whisk in cocoa powder and gelatin mixture until blended and both the cocoa powder and gelatin are dissolved. Whisk in sour cream and almond extract until blended.

Ladle or pour mixture into 8 ¾-cup custard cups, ramekins, or small molds. Loosely cover with plastic wrap and chill 4 hours or up to overnight.

Working over a medium bowl, cut oranges between membranes with a small sharp knife to release segments and their juices into the bowl. Add the berries and toss to combine. Chill until ready to serve.

Cut around edges of each panna cotta to loosen. Set each cup in shallow bowl of hot water for 10 seconds. Immediately invert each onto a plate. Serve with fruit and sprinkle plates with amaretti. Makes 8 servings.

¼ cup dark rum

2⅛ teaspoons unflavored gelatin

2¼ cups evaporated fat-free milk (from 2 12-ounce cans)

½ cup packed light brown sugar

½ cup unsweetened cocoa powder (not Dutch process), sifted

1 cup reduced-fat (not fat-free) sour cream

½ teaspoon almond extract

2 large navel oranges, peel and white pith removed

2 cups assorted berries

1 cup coarsely chopped amaretti cookies (Italian macaroons)

Butter Pecan Panna Cotta

This easy dessert has it all—a rich, buttery custard and a glistening, pecan-studded butterscotch topping—except for the high fat and calories you might expect.

Place water in small bowl. Sprinkle gelatin over water. Let stand 5 minutes to soften gelatin.

Place evaporated milk and brown sugar in medium saucepan. Bring to a simmer over medium-high heat, stirring until sugar is dissolved; remove from heat. Whisk in gelatin mixture until blended and gelatin is dissolved. Whisk in buttermilk until blended.

Ladle or pour mixture into 8 ¾-cup custard cups, ramekins, or small molds. Loosely cover with plastic wrap and chill 4 hours or up to overnight.

Just before serving, place the butterscotch ice cream topping in a small microwavable bowl. Microwave 10–15 seconds on high, just until loose enough to stir. Stir in pecans. Cut around edges of each panna cotta to loosen. Set each cup in shallow bowl of hot water for 10 seconds. Immediately invert each onto a plate. Drizzle with butterscotch-pecan sauce. Makes 8 servings.

¼ cup water

2 teaspoons unflavored gelatin

1 12-ounce can evaporated fat-free milk

½ cup packed light brown sugar

2 cups low-fat buttermilk

¾ cup reduced-fat butterscotch ice cream topping

½ cup chopped, lightly toasted pecans

Five-Herb Panna Cotta

This herb-infused confection is a springtime departure from traditional desserts. One of its many attributes is that it is exquisitely delicious with most any combination of fresh herbs, so enjoy experimenting with whatever is abundant in the garden or from the farmer's market. Fresh berries are the ideal, understated accompaniment.

Bring evaporated milk, sugar, and all of the herb sprigs to simmer in heavy, medium saucepan over medium-high heat; remove from heat. Let steep, covered, 20 minutes.

Meanwhile, place water in small bowl. Sprinkle gelatin over water. Let stand 5 minutes to soften gelatin.

Remove herb sprigs from milk mixture with a slotted spoon. Rewarm milk 2–3 minutes over low heat until very warm. Whisk in gelatin mixture until gelatin is melted. Whisk in sour cream.

Ladle or pour mixture into 8 ¾-cup custard cups, ramekins, or small molds. Loosely cover with plastic wrap and chill 4 hours or up to overnight.

Cut around edges of each panna cotta to loosen. Set each cup in shallow bowl of hot water for 10 seconds. Immediately invert each onto a plate. Serve with fresh berries. Makes 8 servings.

2 cups cannned evaporated fat-free milk (from 2 12-ounce cans)

½ cup sugar

1 (3- to 4-inch) fresh lemon balm sprig

1 (3- to 4-inch) fresh basil sprig

1 (3- to 4-inch) fresh tarragon sprig

1 (3- to 4-inch) fresh mint sprig

1 (3- to 4-inch) fresh lavender sprig

¼ cup water

2 teaspoons unflavored gelatin

1½ cups reduced-fat (not fat-free) sour cream

2 cups fresh berries

Café Brulot Panna Cotta

The traditional New Orleans flaming brew of coffee, spices, orange and lemon peel, and brandy has never been more delicious than in this swanky panna cotta concoction (which tastes anything but light).

Place 4 tablespoons brandy in small bowl. Sprinkle gelatin over brandy. Let stand 5 minutes to soften gelatin.

Place evaporated milk, brown sugar, lemon zest, and orange zest in medium saucepan. Bring to a simmer over medium-high heat, stirring until sugar is dissolved; remove from heat. Whisk in espresso powder and gelatin mixture until blended and gelatin is dissolved. Whisk in sour cream, cinnamon, and cloves until blended.

Ladle or pour mixture into 8 ¾-cup custard cups, ramekins, or small molds. Loosely cover with plastic wrap and chill 4 hours or up to overnight.

Cut around edges of each panna cotta to loosen. Set each cup in shallow bowl of hot water for 10 seconds. Immediately invert each onto a plate. Drizzle with remaining 2 tablespoons brandy and, if desired, garnish with strips of citrus zest. Makes 8 servings.

6 tablespoons brandy, divided use

2⅛ teaspoons unflavored gelatin

2 cups canned evaporated fat-free milk (from 2 12-ounce cans)

½ cup packed light brown sugar

1 teaspoon finely grated lemon zest

1 teaspoon finely grated orange zest

2½ teaspoons instant coffee or espresso powder

1¼ cups reduced-fat (not fat-free) sour cream

½ teaspoon ground cinnamon

⅛ teaspoon ground cloves

Optional garnishes: strips of orange and/or lemon zest (peeled with vegetable peeler)

Enlightened Panna Cotta

Blueberry Cheesecake Panna Cotta

The rich, cheesecake flavor of this panna cotta—achieved with a smooth blend of cottage cheese and buttermilk—belies its light profile. Find your thrill with the quick-to-prepare blueberry sauce, which allows the deeply flavorful fruit to shine.

1½ cups fat-free cottage cheese
1¼ cups low-fat buttermilk
1 teaspoon vanilla extract
2 teaspoons unflavored gelatin
¾ cup low-fat milk
½ cup powdered sugar
1 recipe Blueberry Sauce (see below)

Place cottage cheese, buttermilk and vanilla in blender or food processor container. Cover and blend until puréed. Set aside momentarily.

In a small saucepan, sprinkle gelatin over the milk. Let stand 5 minutes to soften gelatin. Cook and stir over low heat until the gelatin is completely dissolved (do not let mixture come to a boil). Whisk in the powdered sugar and the cottage cheese mixture until blended.

Ladle or pour mixture into 8 ¾-cup custard cups, ramekins, or small molds. Loosely cover with plastic wrap and chill 4 hours or up to overnight.

Cut around edges of each panna cotta to loosen. Set each cup in shallow bowl of hot water for 10 seconds. Immediately invert onto plate. Spoon blueberry sauce around each panna cotta. Makes 8 servings.

BLUEBERRY SAUCE

2 cups fresh blueberries, divided use
2½ tablespoons sugar
½ teaspoon cornstarch
1 teaspoon grated lemon zest

In large saucepan, combine 1½ cups blueberries, sugar, cornstarch, and lemon zest. Set over moderately low heat and stir gently until sugar dissolves. Raise heat to moderately high and boil, stirring occasionally, for 3 minutes. Remove from heat and gently stir in remaining blueberries. Cool completely.

Lime Panna Cotta

WITH TROPICAL CARAMEL SAUCE

This sublimely lime panna cotta is mellowed with a touch of vanilla and partnered with an island-inspired caramel sauce. So easy to make, and figure friendly to boot, it will surely become a summer entertaining standby.

Place lime juice in small bowl. Sprinkle gelatin over juice. Let stand 5 minutes to soften gelatin.

Place evaporated milk, sugar, and 1 teaspoon lime zest in medium saucepan. Bring to a simmer over medium-high heat, stirring until sugar is dissolved; remove from heat. Whisk in gelatin mixture until blended and gelatin is dissolved. Whisk in sour cream and vanilla until blended.

Ladle or pour mixture into 8 ¾-cup custard cups, ramekins, or small molds. Loosely cover with plastic wrap and chill 4 hours or up to overnight.

Just before serving, place the caramel ice cream topping and rum in a small microwavable bowl. Microwave 10–15 seconds on high just until loose enough to stir. Stir in ½ teaspoon lime zest. Cut around edges of each panna cotta to loosen. Set each cup in shallow bowl of hot water for 10 seconds. Immediately invert each onto a plate. Drizzle with tropical caramel sauce. Makes 8 servings.

¼ cup fresh lime juice

2 teaspoons unflavored gelatin

1 12-ounce can evaporated fat-free milk

½ cup sugar

1 teaspoon grated lime zest

1¾ cups reduced-fat (not fat-free) sour cream

1 teaspoon vanilla extract

TROPICAL CARAMEL SAUCE

¾ cup premium reduced-fat caramel ice cream topping

1 tablespoon dark rum

½ teaspoon grated lime zest

Yogurt Panna Cotta

WITH HONEYDEW

This smooth and slightly tart yogurt panna cotta is utterly dependent on the ripeness of the fruit: be picky and opt for only a perfectly ripe, aromatic melon to produce the ambrosial combination of flavors you're after.

Place water in small bowl. Sprinkle gelatin over water. Let stand 5 minutes to soften gelatin.

Place evaporated milk and sugar in medium saucepan. Bring to a simmer over medium-high heat, stirring until sugar is dissolved; remove from heat. Whisk in gelatin mixture until blended and gelatin is dissolved. Whisk in yogurt, vanilla, and cardamom until blended.

Ladle or pour mixture into 8 ¾-cup custard cups, ramekins, or small molds. Loosely cover with plastic wrap and chill 4 hours or up to overnight.

Cut around edges of each panna cotta to loosen. Set each cup in shallow bowl of hot water for 10 seconds. Immediately invert each onto a plate. Serve with honeydew salsa. Makes 8 servings.

¼ cup water
2⅛ teaspoons unflavored gelatin
1 12-ounce can evaporated fat-free milk
½ cup sugar
2 cups low-fat yogurt
1 teaspoon vanilla extract
¼ teaspoon ground cardamom
1 recipe Honeydew Salsa (see below)

HONEYDEW SALSA

2 cups diced honeydew melon (small dice, about ¼-inch)
1 tablespoon fresh lime juice
1 tablespoon chopped fresh basil or mint leaves
1 tablespoon honey

In a medium bowl combine the honeydew, lime juice, chopped herbs, and honey. Chill until ready to use.

Linzer Panna Cotta

This play of almonds, raspberries, citrus, and delicate hints of spice—the flavor profile of classic Austrian Linzer tart—goes beautifully with steaming espresso.

Place evaporated milk in medium saucepan. Sprinkle gelatin over milk. Let stand 5 minutes to soften gelatin.

Set heat under saucepan to medium and stir until gelatin dissolves, about 5 minutes (do not boil). Add brown sugar and whisk until sugar dissolves, about 2 minutes. Remove from heat and whisk in sour cream, almond extract, vanilla, and cinnamon.

Ladle or pour mixture into 8 ¾-cup custard cups, ramekins, or small molds. Loosely cover with plastic wrap and chill 4 hours or up to overnight.

In a small saucepan, melt the jam with the water and lemon zest, stirring until blended. Remove from heat and let cool to room temperature.

Cut around edges of each panna cotta to loosen. Set each cup in shallow bowl of hot water for 10 seconds. Immediately invert each onto a plate. Drizzle raspberry sauce over and around each panna cotta and sprinkle with some of the almonds. Makes 8 servings.

2 cups evaporated fat-free milk (from 2 12-ounce cans)

2⅛ teaspoons unflavored gelatin

½ cup firmly packed light brown sugar

1½ cups reduced-fat (not fat-free) sour cream

¾ teaspoon pure almond extract

½ teaspoon vanilla extract

⅛ teaspoon ground cinnamon

¾ cup seedless raspberry jam

3 tablespoons water

1 teaspoon grated lemon zest

⅓ cup sliced almonds, lightly toasted

Enlightened Panna Cotta

Grasshopper Panna Cotta

Crème de cacao is a brown or clear ("white") chocolate-flavored liqueur made from the cacao bean. It provides just the right kick in this panna cotta version of the classic cocktail.

Place crème de cacao in small bowl. Sprinkle gelatin over liqueur. Let stand 5 minutes to soften gelatin.

Place evaporated milk and sugar in medium saucepan. Bring to a simmer over medium-high heat, stirring until sugar is dissolved; remove from heat. Whisk in gelatin mixture until blended and gelatin is dissolved. Whisk in sour cream, peppermint extract, and food coloring until blended.

Ladle or pour mixture into 8 ¾-cup custard cups, ramekins, or small molds. Loosely cover with plastic wrap and chill 4 hours or up to overnight.

Cut around edges of each panna cotta to loosen. Set each cup in shallow bowl of hot water for 10 seconds. Immediately invert each onto a plate. Drizzle with dark chocolate sauce. Makes 8 servings.

¼ cup white crème de cacao

2⅛ teaspoons unflavored gelatin

1¾ cups evaporated fat-free milk (from 2 12-ounce cans)

½ cup sugar

1½ cups reduced-fat (not fat-free) sour cream

1 teaspoon peppermint extract

1–2 drops green food coloring (to tint pale green)

1 recipe Dark Chocolate Sauce (see page 100)

Enlightened Panna Cotta

Chapter 6

SAVORY

PANNA COTTA

Butternut Squash Panna Cotta

WITH FRESH SAGE AND PARMESAN

The velvety squash custard would be tempting enough—even without the complements of fruity olive oil, nutty-sweet Parmesan cheese, and the surprise of sage. To further streamline the preparation, consider using frozen cooked squash purée. It's sold in 24-ounce packages in the grocery freezer section.

Put oven rack in middle position and preheat oven to 400°F. Roast squash, cut sides down, in a lightly oiled shallow baking pan until neck is tender, about 1 hour. Remove from oven and cool squash to warm.

Scoop flesh from squash, discarding skin, and purée in a food processor until smooth, about 45 seconds. Set aside 1¼ cups of the purée.

Place broth in medium saucepan. Sprinkle gelatin over. Let stand 5 minutes to soften gelatin. Cook and stir over low heat until the gelatin is completely dissolved. Whisk in the 1¼ cups of squash purée along with the cream, grated Parmesan, rubbed sage, and white pepper. Season with salt to taste.

Ladle or pour mixture into 6 ¾-cup custard cups, ramekins, or small molds that have been lightly sprayed with nonstick cooking spray. Loosely cover with plastic wrap and chill 4 hours or up to overnight.

Cut around edges of each panna cotta to loosen. Set each cup in shallow bowl of hot water for 10 seconds. Immediately invert onto plate. Toss arugula with olive oil in a medium bowl to coat. Season with salt and pepper to taste, then divide among the plates of panna cotta. Garnish with fresh sage leaves and Parmesan shavings. Makes 6 servings.

1 2-pound butternut squash, halved lengthwise and seeded
1 cup canned vegetable broth
2¾ teaspoons unflavored gelatin
1¼ cups half and half
½ cup finely grated Parmesan cheese
1¾ teaspoons dry rubbed sage
½ teaspoon white pepper
3 cups baby arugula leaves
1 tablespoon extra-virgin olive oil
Garnish: fresh sage leaves & Parmesan cheese shavings

Feta Panna Cotta

WITH WATERMELON-MINT SALSA

Feta and watermelon? Oh yes. The combination may sound unusual, but the marriage of flavors—the salty tang of cheese mellowed by the sweet brightness of the melon—is definitely a Mediterranean match made in heaven.

Purée feta, sour cream, and garlic in a food processor until smooth. Set aside momentarily.

Combine water and lemon juice in small bowl. Sprinkle gelatin over. Let stand 5 minutes to soften gelatin.

Bring cream just to a simmer in a medium heavy saucepan over moderate heat. Add gelatin mixture and whisk until gelatin is dissolved. Whisk in feta mixture until mixture is blended and smooth. Season with salt to taste.

Ladle or pour mixture into 6 ¾-cup custard cups, ramekins, or small molds. Loosely cover with plastic wrap and chill 4 hours or up to overnight.

Cut around edges of each panna cotta to loosen. Set each cup in shallow bowl of hot water for 10 seconds. Immediately invert each onto a plate. Serve with watermelon-mint salsa and garnish with mint sprigs, if desired. Makes 6 servings.

8 ounces feta cheese, coarsely crumbled
¾ cup sour cream
1 teaspoon minced garlic
2 tablespoons water
2 tablespoons fresh lemon juice
1¾ teaspoons unflavored gelatin
1 cup light cream (half and half)
1 recipe Watermelon-Mint Salsa (see below)
Optional: 6 mint sprigs

WATERMELON-MINT SALSA

3 tablespoons fresh lime juice
1 tablespoon packed light brown sugar
3 cups chopped seeded watermelon
⅓ cup chopped red onion
3 tablespoons thinly sliced fresh mint

Whisk lime juice and brown sugar in large bowl until sugar dissolves. Add watermelon, red onion, and mint and toss gently to combine. Season with salt and pepper. (Can be prepared 2 hours ahead. Cover and chill.)

Porcini Panna Cotta

WITH ROASTED WILD MUSHROOMS

Time to get fancy: this chic first course is a cook's dream because both the custard and the roasted mushrooms can be made ahead. Best of all, both preparations taste even better the next day.

Place the rinsed porcinis and ¾ cup water in a small saucepan set over high heat and bring to a boil. Lower heat to a simmer and cook until porcinis are very soft and liquid has reduced to ½ cup. Remove from heat; cool. When cooled, remove porcinis from liquid with a fine mesh sieve, reserving liquid.

In a small sauté pan melt the butter over medium-high heat. Add the shallots and sauté until softened, about 3 minutes. Add garlic and thyme and cook another minute. Transfer to the bowl of a food processor; add reserved mushroom liquid and porcinis and process until smooth. Set aside momentarily.

Place ½ cup cream in a medium saucepan. Sprinkle gelatin over cream. Let stand 5 minutes to soften gelatin. Bring mixture to a simmer, whisking until gelatin is dissolved. Remove from heat and whisk in remaining cream, porcini mixture, nutmeg, and Parmesan cheese until blended and smooth. Season with salt to taste.

Ladle or pour mixture into 6 ¾-cup custard cups, ramekins, or small molds. Loosely cover with plastic wrap and chill 4 hours or up to overnight.

Cut around edges of each panna cotta to loosen. Set each cup in shallow bowl of hot water for 10 seconds. Immediately invert each onto a plate. Serve with cooled roasted mushrooms and garnish with thyme sprigs. Makes 6 servings.

2 ounces dried porcini mushrooms, rinsed under cold water

¾ cup water

1½ tablespoons butter

¼ cup minced shallots

3 cloves garlic, minced

2 teaspoons finely chopped thyme

1½ cups heavy cream

1½ teaspoons unflavored gelatin

Pinch of freshly grated nutmeg

½ cup freshly grated Parmesan cheese

1 recipe Roasted Wild Mushrooms (see next page)

Garnish: 6 fresh thyme sprigs

ROASTED WILD MUSHROOMS

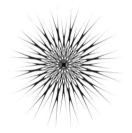

1¼ pounds assorted wild
mushrooms, cleaned

4 cloves garlic, thinly sliced

¼ cup olive oil

1 tablespoon Worcestershire sauce

1 tablespoon chopped fresh thyme leaves

Preheat oven to 375°F. Combine the mushrooms and garlic in a large roasting pan, add
the olive oil and freshly ground pepper to taste
and stir to combine. Roast in the oven until
golden brown and all of the liquid has evaporated, 25–30 minutes, stirring occasionally.
Remove from the oven and stir in the Worcestershire, salt to taste, and chopped thyme.
Cool to room temperature to serve with the
panna cotta.

Savory Panna Cotta

Asparagus Panna Cotta

If any food sings spring, it's asparagus. The very name, related to the Greek word meaning to swell or burst forth, describes the season. I devised this panna cotta to showcase its magnificence, in both flavor and form.

Cut tips from 12 asparagus 1½ inches from top and halve tips lengthwise if thick. Reserve for garnish. Cut stalks and all remaining asparagus into ½-inch pieces.

Cook onion in the butter in a medium, heavy pot over moderately low heat, stirring, until softened. Add asparagus pieces and salt and pepper to taste, then cook, stirring, 5 minutes. Add broth and simmer, covered, until asparagus is very tender, 15–20 minutes.

While asparagus stalks simmer, cook reserved asparagus tips in boiling salted water until just tender, 3–4 minutes, then drain. Cover and chill until ready to use.

Combine water and lemon juice in small bowl. Sprinkle gelatin over mixture. Let stand 5 minutes to soften gelatin.

Purée asparagus pieces (not tips) in batches in a blender until smooth, transferring to a bowl (use caution when blending hot liquids). Measure out 1 cup of purée (use excess for other use) and return to pot. Add gelatin mixture, whisking until gelatin is dissolved. Whisk in cream, white pepper, and nutmeg. Season with salt to taste.

Ladle or pour mixture into 6 ¾-cup custard cups, ramekins, or small molds that have been lightly sprayed with nonstick cooking spray. Loosely cover with plastic wrap and chill 4 hours or up to overnight.

Cut around edges of each panna cotta to loosen. Set each cup in shallow bowl of hot water for 10 seconds. Immediately invert each onto the side of a plate. Garnish each panna cotta with a small spoonful of the sour cream and 2 asparagus tips. Makes 6 servings.

1 pound asparagus, ends trimmed
1 cup chopped onion
1 tablespoon unsalted butter
1¼ cups low-sodium chicken broth
2 tablespoons water
2 teaspoons fresh lemon juice
1¾ teaspoons unflavored gelatin
1½ cups heavy whipping cream
¼ teaspoon ground white pepper
⅛ teaspoon ground nutmeg
⅓ cup sour cream

Summer Corn Panna Cotta

WITH FRESH CRAB

This recipe is meant for warm, late summer days when the corn is sweet and fresh basil is at its finest. The light vibrant flavors will revive your spirits. In a pinch, canned lump crabmeat may be substituted for the fresh crabmeat.

Melt butter in a medium saucepan over medium-high heat. Add onion and corn, stirring until the onions are slightly softened (do not let brown). Stir in ½ cup wine; continue cooking until wine is absorbed. Add cream, salt, and fresh pepper to taste. Heat until cream just starts to bubble, then turn heat down and simmer for 5 minutes.

Transfer mixture to a food processor in small batches and purée. Strain through a mesh sieve using a rubber spatula; discard solids.

Place remaining ¼ cup wine in small bowl. Sprinkle gelatin over wine. Let stand 5 minutes to soften gelatin. Season with salt and pepper to taste.

Return corn purée to saucepan. Rewarm until very warm but not hot. Whisk gelatin mixture into corn purée until gelatin is dissolved.

Ladle or pour mixture into 6 ¾-cup custard cups, ramekins, or small molds that have been lightly sprayed with nonstick cooking spray. Loosely cover with plastic wrap and chill 4 hours or up to overnight.

In a medium bowl gently toss together the crabmeat, basil, and olive oil. Season with salt and pepper to taste.

Cut around edges of each panna cotta to loosen. Set each cup in shallow bowl of hot water for 10 seconds. Immediately invert each onto a plate and top with some of the crabmeat. Makes 6 servings.

1 tablespoon unsalted butter
1 cup chopped onion
3 cups frozen corn kernels
¾ cup dry white wine, divided use
2 cups heavy whipping cream
2¼ teaspoons unflavored gelatin
12 ounces lump crabmeat, picked over
¼ cup packed fresh basil, cut into slivers or chiffonade
1½ tablespoons extra-virgin olive oil

Savory Panna Cotta

Goat Cheese Panna Cotta

WITH ARUGULA-ROASTED BEET SALAD

The peppery mustard flavor of arugula and earthy sweetness of roasted beets team up with goat cheese in this stunning interpretation of a favorite combination of flavors. Be sure to select a goat cheese with an assertive tang, as well as a creamy (as opposed to dry) consistency, for optimal melting and a velvety texture.

Place water in small bowl. Sprinkle gelatin over water. Let stand 5 minutes to soften gelatin.

Place the heavy cream in medium saucepan. Bring to a simmer over medium-high heat; remove from heat. Whisk in gelatin mixture until blended and gelatin is dissolved. Whisk in thyme and goat cheese until blended and smooth. Whisk in sour cream. Season with salt and pepper to taste.

Ladle or pour mixture into 6 ¾-cup custard cups, ramekins, or small molds. Loosely cover with plastic wrap and chill 4 hours or up to overnight.

Cut around edges of each panna cotta to loosen. Set each cup in shallow bowl of hot water for 10 seconds. Immediately invert each onto the side of a salad plate. Divide salad among 6 plates and scatter the walnuts on top. Makes 6 servings.

3 tablespoons water
1½ teaspoons unflavored gelatin
1¼ cups heavy whipping cream
2 teaspoons finely chopped fresh thyme
8 ounces goat cheese, crumbled
½ cup sour cream
1 recipe Arugula-Roasted Beet Salad

ARUGULA-ROASTED BEET SALAD

1 bunch medium beets (about ¾ pounds)
2 tablespoons balsamic vinegar
⅓ cup extra-virgin olive oil
6 cups fresh arugula
1 firm-ripe Haas avocado, peeled, pitted, and diced
½ cup walnuts, toasted, coarsely chopped

Line a baking sheet with foil. Preheat the oven to 450°F.

Put the beets in a saucepan with water to cover and season generously with salt. Bring to a boil over high heat and cook until fork-tender, about 20 minutes. When the beets are cool enough to handle, peel and cut into bite-sized wedges.

In a medium bowl whisk the vinegar and olive oil in a slow steady stream to make a dressing. Season with salt & pepper to taste. Toss the cut beets in the dressing; set aside to marinate for at least 15 minutes or up to 2 hours. Toss the arugula with the beets and avocado.

Avocado Panna Cotta

WITH ANCHO CREAM

The lush, velvety texture of fresh avocados produces an exceptionally smooth panna cotta. The ancho chiles in the accompanying cream are dried poblanos. They are available at some supermarkets, at specialty foods stores, and at Latin markets.

Place broth in small bowl. Sprinkle gelatin over broth. Let stand 5 minutes to soften gelatin.

Bring the cream and lime zest to simmer in heavy, medium saucepan set over medium-high heat. Remove from heat. Add gelatin mixture, whisking until gelatin is dissolved. Set aside momentarily.

Quarter, pit, and peel avocados. Purée the avocados with the lime juice, cayenne, garlic, and cumin in a food processor until smooth. Add ½ cup of cream mixture; blend well. Add avocado mixture to saucepan with cream, whisking until blended. Season with salt and pepper to taste.

Ladle or pour mixture into 6 ¾-cup custard cups, ramekins, or small molds that have been lightly sprayed with nonstick cooking spray. Loosely cover with plastic wrap and chill 4 hours or up to overnight.

Cut around edges of each panna cotta to loosen. Set each cup in shallow bowl of hot water for 10 seconds. Immediately invert each onto a plate. Drizzle plates with ancho cream. Makes 6 servings.

⅓ cup canned vegetable broth

2 teaspoons unflavored gelatin

1¾ cups heavy whipping cream

1 teaspoon very finely grated lime zest

2 large ripe avocados

2 tablespoons fresh lime juice

¼ teaspoon cayenne pepper

1 clove garlic, peeled

½ teaspoon ground cumin

ANCHO CREAM

1 large dried ancho chile, halved, stem and seeds removed

⅔ cup whipping cream

Dash of ground cinnamon

Heat small skillet over medium heat. Add chile and toast the pieces on each side until pliable and aromatic, turning occasionally, about 2 minutes. Transfer chile to small bowl and add hot water just to cover. Soak until soft, about 30 minutes. Drain water; finely mince chile. Place whipping cream in a small bowl; whisk in 2 tablespoons minced ancho and the cinnamon. Season with salt to taste. Chill until ready to use.

Cauliflower Panna Cotta

WITH WHITE TRUFFLE OIL

Dressed in lusty white truffle oil, this elegant first course has few rivals.

Cook cauliflower and garlic in a medium saucepan of boiling salted water until very tender, about 5–7 minutes; drain in a colander. Purée cauliflower and garlic in a food processor until smooth. Measure ¾ cup of the purée (reserve remaining purée for another use). Place the ¾ cup purée back in saucepan and whisk in heavy cream.

Place water in small bowl. Sprinkle gelatin over water. Let stand 5 minutes to soften gelatin.

Rewarm cauliflower mixture over medium heat until very warm. Whisk in gelatin mixture until blended and smooth. Whisk in sour cream and nutmeg. Season with salt and pepper to taste.

Ladle or pour mixture into 6 ¾-cup custard cups, ramekins, or small molds that have been lightly sprayed with nonstick cooking spray. Loosely cover with plastic wrap and chill 4 hours or up to overnight.

Cut around edges of each panna cotta to loosen. Set each cup in shallow bowl of hot water for 10 seconds. Immediately invert each onto the side of a salad plate. Toss watercress with 1 tablespoon of the truffle oil; season with salt and pepper to taste. Arrange ½ cup watercress around each panna cotta and drizzle custards with remaining tablespoon truffle oil. Makes 6 servings.

2 cups chopped cauliflower
4 garlic cloves, peeled
1 cup heavy whipping cream
3 tablespoons water
1½ teaspoons unflavored gelatin
⅓ cup sour cream
⅛ teaspoon ground nutmeg
2 tablespoons white truffle oil
3 cups tender watercress sprigs

Cook's note: White truffle oil is available at Italian markets, many specialty foods stores, and some supermarkets.

Queso Fresco Panna Cotta

WITH CHIMICHURRI & CHERRY TOMATOES

Here the piquancy of chimichurri—a fresh herb, olive oil, and vinegar sauce typical of Argentinean cuisine—meets the mellowness of queso fresco—a soft, fresh, Mexican cheese—with stellar results. The addition of summer-ripe cherry tomatoes to each plate makes this a stunning starter.

Purée queso fresco, sour cream, and cumin in a food processor until smooth. Set aside momentarily.

Place water in small bowl. Sprinkle gelatin over. Let stand 5 minutes to soften gelatin.

Bring cream just to a simmer in a heavy, medium saucepan over moderate heat. Add gelatin mixture and whisk until dissolved. Whisk in queso mixture until mixture is blended and smooth. Season with salt and pepper to taste.

Ladle or pour mixture into 6 ¾-cup custard cups, ramekins, or small molds. Loosely cover with plastic wrap and chill 4 hours or up to overnight.

Cut around edges of each panna cotta to loosen. Set each cup in shallow bowl of hot water for 10 seconds. Immediately invert each onto the side of a salad plate. Divide cherry tomatoes among the plates; drizzle panna cotta with chimichurri. Makes 6 servings.

6 ounces queso fresco or feta cheese
½ cup sour cream
1 teaspoon ground cumin
3 tablespoons water
1¾ teaspoons unflavored gelatin
1⅓ cups heavy whipping cream
2 cups mixed color (e.g., red, orange, and yellow) cherry tomatoes, halved
1 recipe Chimichurri (see below)

CHIMICHURRI

1 cup packed fresh flat leaf parsley
½ cup extra virgin olive oil
¼ cup red wine vinegar
¼ cup packed fresh cilantro
2 garlic cloves, peeled
½ teaspoon ground cumin
¼ teaspoon dried crushed red pepper
½ teaspoon salt

Purée all ingredients in food processor or blender. Transfer to a small bowl and cover. Refrigerate until ready to serve.

Fresh Chive Panna Cotta

WITH CAVIAR & CROSTINI

A fresh lemon and herb-infused custard, crunchy crostini, and the sophisticated saltiness of caviar add up to one glam first course.

Place heavy cream, lemon zest, and ½ cup chives in medium saucepan. Bring to a simmer over medium-high heat; remove from heat. Let steep, covered, 15 minutes.

Meanwhile, place water in small bowl. Sprinkle gelatin over water. Let stand 5 minutes to soften gelatin.

Remove lemon zest from saucepan. Rewarm cream mixture 2–3 minutes until very warm but not hot. Whisk in white pepper, and gelatin mixture until blended and gelatin is dissolved. Whisk in sour cream until blended. Season with salt to taste.

Ladle or pour mixture into 6 ¾-cup custard cups, ramekins, or small molds. Loosely cover with plastic wrap and chill 4 hours or up to overnight.

Cut around edges of each panna cotta to loosen. Set each cup in shallow bowl of hot water for 10 seconds. Immediately invert each onto a plate. Top each panna cotta with a dollop of caviar and sprinkle plates with chives. Arrange the crostini on the plates. Makes 6 servings.

2 cups heavy whipping cream

3 2x½-inch strips lemon zest

½ cup plus 2 tablespoons finely chopped fresh chives, divided use

3 tablespoons water

1¾ teaspoons unflavored gelatin

1¼ teaspoons salt

¼ teaspoon ground white pepper

½ cup sour cream

3 ounces American-farmed caviar

FRENCH BREAD CROSTINI

½ of a 12-inch loaf French baguette

3 tablespoons extra-virgin olive oil

¼ teaspoon coarse salt

⅛ teaspoon freshly ground black pepper

Preheat oven to 400°F. Cut bread into ¼-inch round or oval slices and place on a baking sheet. Brush 1 side of each slice with the olive oil and lightly season with the salt and pepper. Bake for 8 minutes or until light golden brown and crispy. Remove from the oven and cool.

Carrot Panna Cotta

WITH DILL PESTO

Packaged baby carrots have never been so refined. As the start to a fine spring meal, the delicate flavor marriage of the sweet carrots and dill signals a sophisticated advent.

Melt butter in heavy, large pot over medium heat. Add carrots and onion; sauté until onion is soft, about 8 minutes. Add garlic and broth; cover and bring to boil. Reduce heat, uncover, and simmer until carrots are tender, about 10 minutes.

Using a slotted spoon transfer carrots and onion to a food processor. Add 1 cup of the cooking broth and purée until very smooth. Measure out 1 cup purée; place in pot (use remaining carrot purée for another use). Whisk in cream. Season with salt and pepper to taste.

Place water in small bowl. Sprinkle gelatin over water. Let stand 5 minutes to soften gelatin.

Reheat carrot mixture, covered, over moderate heat, stirring occasionally, until very warm. Remove from heat and whisk in gelatin until dissolved.

Ladle or pour mixture into 6 ¾-cup custard cups, ramekins, or small molds that have been lightly sprayed with nonstick cooking spray. Loosely cover with plastic wrap and chill 4 hours or up to overnight.

Cut around edges of each panna cotta to loosen. Set each cup in shallow bowl of hot water for 10 seconds. Immediately invert each onto the side of a salad plate. Serve panna cotta with a small dollop of dill pesto. Makes 6 servings.

1 tablespoon butter
1 1-pound bag classic-cut peeled baby carrots
¾ cup chopped onion
1 clove garlic, minced
2½ cups low-sodium chicken broth
1½ cups heavy whipping cream
2 tablespoons water
2 teaspoons unflavored gelatin

DILL PESTO

1 cup packed coarsely chopped fresh dill
2 tablespoons pine nuts
3 tablespoons olive oil

Combine fresh dill and pine nuts in processor and chop finely using on/off turns. With processor running, slowly add olive oil and process until well blended. Season to taste with salt and pepper. Cover and refrigerate until ready to use.

Celeriae-Apple Panna Cotta

WITH BROWNED BUTTER VINAIGRETTE

Knobby and brown, celeriac (also known as celery root) may be one of the ugliest vegetables around. But its beautiful, earthy sweetness belies its exterior. Together with the crisp flavor of apple, it makes for a rather extraordinary panna cotta. The browned butter vinaigrette lends a nutty, piquant contrast, making this a superb first course choice for your next autumn supper party.

Peel celery root with a sharp knife, then cut into 1-inch cubes. Peel and core apple, then cut into 1-inch pieces.

Melt butter in a heavy, medium pot over moderately low heat, then add celery root, and apples, and stir to coat with butter. Cover with a tight-fitting lid and cook (without adding liquid), stirring occasionally, until celery root is tender, about 45–50 minutes.

Purée mixture in a food processor until smooth. Measure out 1 cup purée; place in pot. (Use remaining purée for another use.) Whisk in cream, white pepper, and nutmeg. Season with salt and pepper to taste.

Place water in small bowl. Sprinkle gelatin over water. Let stand 5 minutes to soften gelatin.

Reheat celery root–apple mixture, covered, over moderate heat, stirring occasionally, until very warm. Remove from heat and whisk in gelatin until dissolved.

Ladle or pour mixture into 6 ¾-cup custard cups, ramekins, or small molds that have been lightly sprayed with nonstick cooking spray.

Loosely cover with plastic wrap and chill 4 hours or up to overnight.

Cut around edges of each panna cotta to loosen. Set each cup in shallow bowl of hot water for 10 seconds. Immediately invert each onto the side of a salad plate. Garnish plates with watercress sprigs and drizzle plates with browned butter vinaigrette. Makes 6 servings.

1⅓ pounds celery root (sometimes called celeriac)
1 medium Gala, Empire, or McIntosh apple
2 tablespoons unsalted butter
1½ cups heavy whipping cream
¼ teaspoon white pepper
¼ teaspoon freshly grated nutmeg
2 tablespoons water
2 teaspoons unflavored gelatin
Garnish: 3 cups tender watercress sprigs
1 recipe Browned Butter Vinaigrette (see next page)

BROWNED BUTTER VINAIGRETTE

5 tablespoons unsalted butter

⅓ cup chopped shallots

¼ cup hazelnuts or almonds,
toasted, chopped

1 tablespoon white wine vinegar

Cook butter in large, nonstick skillet over medium heat until deep golden brown and most of foam subsides, stirring frequently, about 4 minutes. Transfer butter to bowl.

Add shallots and hazelnuts to skillet; stir 30 seconds. Remove skillet from heat. Add browned butter and vinegar; stir to blend. Season vinaigrette with salt and pepper.

Savory Panna Cotta

Gorgonzola Panna Cotta

WITH RED CURRANT GASTRIQUE AND CRISPY PROSCIUTTO

As festive as beautifully wrapped holiday packages, each panna cotta is enrobed in a quickly-crafted red currant gastrique and topped with a sprinkle of pan-fried crispy prosciutto. The miniature custards derive their flavor from an irresistible combination of Gorgonzola, cream, and Marsala, delicately spiced with nutmeg. A delightful starter course, the panna cotta, gastrique, and crispy prosciutto can be made up to a day ahead of time and then assembled in minutes just before serving.

Place Marsala in small bowl. Sprinkle gelatin over Marsala. Let stand 5 minutes to soften gelatin.

Bring cream just to a simmer in a medium heavy saucepan over moderate heat. Add Gorgonzola and whisk until just melted. Remove from heat and add gelatin mixture, whisking until gelatin is dissolved. Season with nutmeg, and salt and pepper to taste.

Ladle or pour mixture into 6 ¾-cup custard cups, ramekins, or small molds. Loosely cover with plastic wrap and chill 4 hours or up to overnight.

Cut around edges of each panna cotta to loosen. Set each cup in shallow bowl of hot water for 10 seconds. Immediately invert onto plate. Garnish with crispy prosciutto and fresh currants. Drizzle gastrique over or beside each panna cotta. Makes 6 servings.

| 3 tablespoons Marsala |
| 1½ teaspoons unflavored gelatin |
| 2 cups heavy whipping cream |
| 1 6-ounce piece of Gorgonzola, cut or crumbled into small pieces |
| Pinch of freshly ground nutmeg |
| 1 recipe Red Currant Gastrique (see below) |
| 1 recipe Crispy Prosciutto (see below) |
| Garnish: 1 cup fresh currants (small, tart red, black, or white variety) |

RED CURRANT GASTRIQUE

| 1 cup red-wine vinegar |
| ¼ cup red currant jelly |

In a small saucepan simmer vinegar until reduced to about ¼ cup. Whisk in red currant jelly, whisking until smooth. Season with salt and pepper to taste. Keep warm, covered.

CRISPY PROSCIUTTO

| 2 tablespoons (¼ stick) butter |
| 3 ounces chopped sliced prosciutto |

Melt butter in medium nonstick skillet over medium heat. Add prosciutto and sauté until crisp, about 6 minutes. Drain on paper towels (may be prepared up to 2 hours in advance).

Appendix: Equipment & Ingredients

Now that I live in a relatively small town, I've come to appreciate cooking supply websites all the more, for acquiring both general and unusual equipment needs as well as less-than-usual ingredients. But having lived in large metropolitan areas, too, I know that it's always handy to know where to locate exactly what you need for a special recipe or technique without having to search high and low. What follows are some of my favorite picks for ingredients and equipment.

www.amazon.com
Search their gourmet foods section and you will find an extensive offering of non-perishable cooking ingredients, from the ordinary (e.g., nuts, dried fruits, spices, and extracts) to the hard-to-find (e.g., chestnut purée, matcha/green tea powder, British golden syrup, rose water). They also sell a large selection of ramekins and molds for making panna cotta.

www.bakerscatalogue.com
The Baker's Catalogue (also available as a printed catalogue) is a leading source for general baking ingredients and equipment. It is an excellent source for more esoteric ingredients such as muscovado sugar and vanilla powder.

www.bedbathandbeyond.com
Both the retail store and the website have an extensive assortment of general cookware. They also sell a variety of pretty ramekins and glassware for molding and serving panna cotta.

www.cooking.com
Very easily my favorite source for ramekins and molds—they have many that are so pretty, you will not want to unmold the panna cotta. It is also an excellent source for general kitchenware.

www.penzeys.com
Penzeys sells an extensive assortment of herbs, spices, and seasonings at excellent prices and in a range of sizes. It is a good source for extracts, vanilla beans, and crystallized ginger, too.

www.surlatable.com
This is another nationwide chain with a very good selection of general cookware, as well as many offerings of ramekins and ¾-cup molds. They have an especially good selection of small, nonstick metal molds (e.g., rounds, ovals, baba-shape) that make unmolding a breeze.

www.williams-sonoma.com
This is the website for the upscale chain of Williams-Sonoma kitchenware stores. You can also request a catalog online. It is an excellent source for general cookware as well as premium ingredients.

Bibliography

Artusi, Pellegrino. *Italian Cook Book*. Adapted from the Italian of Pellegrino Artusi by Olga Ragusa. New York: S. F. Vanni, 1940.

Boni, Ada. *The Talisman Italian Cook Book*. Translated and augmented by Matilde Pei. Introduction by Mario A. Pei. Special edition printed for Ronzoni Macaroni Co., Inc. New York: Crown Publishers, 1955.

Corrado, Vincenzo. *Il Couco Galante*. Di F. Vincenzo Corrado. 5th ed. Napoli: dalla Stamperia Orsiniana, Presso i Fratelli Terres, 1801.

David, Elizabeth. *Italian Food*. New York: Knopf, 1958.

Hammond, Richard. *Eating in Italy: A Pocket Guide to Italian Food and Restaurants*. New York: Scribner, 1957.

Hazan, Marcella. *The Classic Italian Cook Book: The Art of Italian Cooking and the Italian Art of Eating*. New York: Harper's Magazine Press, 1973.

Il Libro della Cucina del Sec. XIV. Bologna: Presso Gaetano Romagnoli, 1863.

Isola, Antonia. *Simple Italian Cookery*. New York: Harper and Brothers, 1912.

L'Arte di far cucina di buon gusto : ove s'insegna con facilità a cucinare ogni sorta di vivande sì in grasso, che in magro ed imbandir mense di nuovo gusto, ed in fine varie preparazioni appartenenti al confetturiere. Torino: Presso Francesco Prato, 1793.

Leonardi, Francesco. *L'Apicio Moderno, Ossia, L'Arte di Apprestare Ogni sorta di Vivande*. Di Francesco Leonardi Romano. Rome or Florence, 1790.

Riello, Mary Carmen. *Italian Cook Book: Contains about 250 Recipes, Learn How to Cook Spaghetti, Broccoli, Artichokes, Ravioli, Meat Balls, etc. the Italian Way*. New Haven, CT: M. Riello, 1936.

Root, Waverley L. *The Food of Italy*. New York: Atheneum, 1971.

Rosselli, Giovanne de. *Epulario: Quale Tratta del Modo de Cucinare Ogni Carne, Ucelli, Pesci, de Ogni Sorte, & Fare Sapori, Torte, & Pastelli, al Modo de Tutte le Prouincie*. Venetia: Appresso gi Heredi di Gioanne Padoano, 1555.

Index

almonds
Chocolate Amaretti with Fresh Fruit, 107
Linzer, 114
Swiss Toblerone, 38
amaretto
White Chocolate Amaretto, 96
apples
Celeriac-Apple with Browned Butter
Vinaigrette, 130
apricots
Yogurt with Poached Apricots, 64
Asparagus, 122
Avocado with Ancho Cream, 125
Baba au Rhum, 86
bananas
Banana with Caramel-Pecan Drizzle, 76
beets
Goat Cheese with Arugula–Roasted Beet
Salad, 124
Bittersweet Chocolate, 22
blackberries
Panna Cotta with Blackberry Compote &
Fresh Sage, 68
blueberries
Blueberry Cheesecake, 111
Lavender with Blueberry Coulis, 28
Butter Pecan, 108
Buttermilk, 69
Butternut Squash with Fresh Sage and
Parmesan, 118

butterscotch
Muscovado Butterscotch, 47
Café Brulot, 110
Cannoli, 44
Cappuccino Layered, 30
caramel
Caramel-Coconut, 45
Chestnut Caramel, 48
Lime with Tropical Caramel Sauce, 112
Winter Spice with Cabernet-Caramel
Sauce, 94
Cardamom with Pistachio-Praline Sauce, 53
Carrot with Dill Pesto, 129
Cauliflower with White Truffle Oil, 126
caviar
Fresh Chive with Caviar & Crostini, 128
Celeriac-Apple with Browned Butter
Vinaigrette, 130
Chai, 50
cheese
Feta with Watermelon-Mint Salsa, 119
Goat Cheese with Arugula–Roasted Beet
Salad, 124
Mascarpone with Dulce de Leche Sauce,
46
Queso Fresco with Chimichurri & Cherry
Tomatoes, 127
Ricotta with Sambuca-Poached Fresh Figs,
93
Roasted Pear with Maytag Blue Cheese, 67
Sweet Goat Cheese with Roasted Plums, 77